PIONEERS & CARETAKERS

A STUDY OF 9 AMERICAN WOMEN NOVELISTS

BY LOUIS AUCHINCLOSS

7546

UNIVERSITY OF MINNESOTA PRESS

Minneapolis

PRINTED IN THE UNITED STATES OF AMERICA AT THE
NORTH CENTRAL PUBLISHING COMPANY, ST. PAUL

 3

Library of Congress Catalog Card Number: 65-17016

Third printing 1966

PUBLISHED IN GREAT BRITAIN, INDIA, AND PAKISTAN BY THE OXFORD
UNIVERSITY PRESS, LONDON, BOMBAY, AND KARACHI, AND IN CANADA BY
THE COPP CLARK PUBLISHING CO. LIMITED, TORONTO

The chapters on Edith Wharton and Ellen Glasgow also appear as
Numbers 12 and 33 in the University of Minnesota
Pamphlets on American Writers

for

Patricia MacManus

*who as friend, reader, and publisher
has been a bulwark of strength and
encouragement from the beginning
of my writing career*

TABLE OF CONTENTS

PIONEERS & CARETAKERS

PIONEERS & CARETAKERS

IN THE MIGRATIONS of tribes the women were responsible for the packing and preservation of the household gods. They have always been the true conservatives, the caretakers of the culture. But because in our nation we have to go back so few decades to get to the Indians, the functions of the caretaker and of the pioneer have become curiously blended. To preserve a bit of the American tradition, one has to preserve a bit of the frontier.

A notable thing about our women writers is that they have struck a more affirmative note than the men. Their darkness is not as dark as that of Dreiser or Lewis or Faulkner or O'Neill, which is not to say that they see America less clearly, but that they may see it more discriminatingly. They have a sharper sense of their stake in the national heritage, and they are always at work to preserve it. They never destroy; they never want the clean sweep. They are conservatives who are always trying to conserve.

Sarah Orne Jewett worried about what we were losing in the simple coastal towns of Maine with their plain talk and plain manners as the men turned from the sea to the factories. Edith Wharton ultimately considered that the sober New York brownstone era of her childhood, the "age of innocence" which had bored her to death as a girl, had nonetheless an integrity, a decorum, and a dignity that

3

later eras might well have used. Willa Cather believed that man's struggle with the soil in the Nebraska prairie life of her early years had brought out the best in him. Ellen Glasgow, even in her most ruthless analysis of the delusions of the South in reconstruction and post-reconstruction days, always felt that the courage and gallantry of the antebellum tradition were indispensable to the good life. And Elizabeth Madox Roberts wrote elegiacally of pioneers and of farms, consciously thinking of the American tradition in terms of the epic.

As we approach our own day, the attitude of the women writers toward our past has become more critical, but it still contains strong elements of nostalgia. Katherine Anne Porter explores the legends of her childhood with a dissecting knife, but she loves these legends. Jean Stafford mocks the inheritors of the Boston traditions, but not the traditions themselves, and Carson McCullers, while showing the terrible decay of the South, has a sentimental attachment for the institutions that are decaying.

To preserve traditions in our own century has become a pretty desperate affair. We are like an ignored committee in a large city rushing from tattered landmark to tattered landmark, futilely protesting a proposed razing to make place for some great glass cube. It is difficult to avoid the strident note, the shrill cry; it is hard to keep from becoming a crank. This has been the danger facing the older novelists considered in this volume and the Waterloo of some.

Sarah Orne Jewett died too early to lock horns with the Rotary Club and the chain store, but Edith Wharton ultimately allowed her irritation to get out of hand and to turn her into a caricature of Sinclair Lewis. Ellen Glasgow as an old woman protested against our century to the point of absurdity, and Elizabeth Madox Roberts in the end became unreadably dull. Willa Cather saved herself only by eschewing what she saw as an era without valor and turning her attention to a more inspiring past.

Later, women novelists penetrated more deeply into the ailments of our time and saw that they consisted of more than the billboard, the assembly line, and the Babbitts. Carson McCullers, Jean Stafford, and Mary McCarthy saw vulgarity as essentially comic and did not magnify it by taking it too seriously. Mrs. McCullers saved her indignation for racial prejudice. Mary McCarthy kept her satirical powers for the confusion of values in the intellectual world and the lack of philosophy in art or teaching. And Katherine Anne Porter, taking the international view of the plight of modern man, located the breeding spot of the fatal virus in pre-Hitler Berlin.

If it seems bold to lump the nine women here treated into a single tradition, consider the common American denominator that runs through the following, each a sample of its author's finest prose: *The Country of the Pointed Firs*, *The Age of Innocence*, *Barren Ground*, *My Ántonia*, and *The Time of Man*. Surely, if one were trying to describe to a European the very essence of the romantic concept of the American dream, one could do no better than supply him with copies of these five novels. And then if he were to proceed to the Miranda stories, to *Boston Adventure*, to *The Ballad of the Sad Café*, and to *Memories of a Catholic Girlhood*, he would find some very interesting qualifications. But in the end the dream would not be destroyed. That is the point. The caretakers, for all their cleaning out, still preserve.

1
SARAH ORNE JEWETT

SARAH ORNE JEWETT, like those other New England spinsters, Emily Dickinson and Amy Lowell, was associated all her life with one house. The big white mansion where she was born in 1849 had been bought by her seafaring grandfather and was one of the finest in South Berwick, Maine. Its interior was embellished with elaborate, dentelated cornices, paneled wainscoting, and arches resting on fluted columns, and it was furnished with Chippendale and Sheraton. For until the Civil War ruined its shipping, Berwick was a prosperous seaport, and the stately, aristocratic life of its first citizens was almost as splendid as that of their counterparts in the South. Miss Jewett was always to feel a deep nostalgia for the departed days of Berwick's glory and never to be quite reconciled to the smoky mills which engaged energies once devoted to the nobler calling of the sea. Her last book, *The Tory Lover*, showing her hometown in revolutionary days, is bathed in the sentiment of a lifetime.

Her father, however, eschewed both the sea and trade; he was a doctor, a beloved general practitioner, and years after his death, when his daughters were beginning to be elderly, they were still known in Berwick as "the Doctor's girls." Sarah used to go with him on his rounds, in both town and country, and seriously entertained the idea of becoming a doctor herself, but periodic attacks of rheumatism prevented fulfillment of this youthful dream. She adopted instead the life of the cultivated young lady of her time: she rode; she sat on committees; she visited friends; she went to Boston for lectures and plays and the sermons of Phillips Brooks. She seems to have had no beaux. "Sarah, was thee ever in love?" John Greenleaf Whittier asked her, and the startled reply was "No! Whatever made you think that?" But to be an old maid of frail body and strong mind was considered a perfectly normal life in the New England of that day.

That she should have started to write early, with contributions to the *Atlantic*, was equally in the New England tradition. She had read passionately in English fiction: in Jane Austen, George Eliot, and Thackeray, particularly the last. *Vanity Fair* was for her Tolstoy and Zola and Turgenev "all rolled in one," and *Pendennis* seemed to her greater than *Anna Karenina* and "more full of true humanity." She had already a reputation as a writer of short stories when her first collection, *Deephaven*, appeared in 1877.

It is curious that Miss Jewett's literary career should have opened and closed with the same literary form: the loose-leaf novel in which a female narrator gives the reader sketches of persons and places in a small Maine village. She must have had a sense from the beginning of the perfect medium for her talent and laid it aside, consciously or not, for the two decades that elapsed between *Deephaven* and *The Country of the Pointed Firs*. It was to take her all of that time to perfect her character sketches of village and farm people, for the difference between success and failure in this delicate art was always a hairline. The danger that stalked her was sentimentality.

There is little to be said about *Deephaven* or about the three small collections of stories and essays that followed it: *Old Friends and New* (1879), *Country By-Ways* (1881), and *The Mate of the Daylight, and Friends Ashore* (1884). They have charm, but it is a pale, wistful charm. In *Deephaven* two young city girls go to spend the summer in a big white house in a Maine coastal village that has just been inherited by one of their families. Their enthusiasm is infectious but superficial; the book is more like a graceful vacation letter than a novel. To do the simple without seeming too simple Miss Jewett needed the skill of Flaubert, and she knew it. As she was later to write: "I copied for him [she was referring to a friend] those two wonderful bits of Flaubert, — 'Écrire la vie ordinaire comme on écrit l'histoire'; and the other, 'Ce n'est pas de faire rire — mais d'agir a la façon de la nature, c'est à dire de faire rêver.' I keep these pinned up on the little drawers at the back of the secretary, for a constant reminder."

She now turned to the conventional novel form with *A Country Doctor* (1884). It is only in parts successful. It fails to hang together, and although this was a common fault in the Victorian novel, it is more noticeable in a book as short as *A Country Doctor*. The elaborate, mysterious Dickensian opening chapters in which Anna's dying mother staggers through the dark with her child to rap at the door of her own mother's living room, where the guests are scaring each other with ghost stories, is dramatically effective, but it is not really necessary to the rest of Anna's tale. We never know just what was wrong with Anna's mother, or why she drank, and the effect of such an inheritance on Anna is, to say the least, cloudy. After Anna has grown up, it is suggested once that she may have renounced marriage because of a distrust of her blood, but in other places it is emphasized that this renunciation is based solely on her conviction that a woman must choose between marriage and a career. Actually, had the novel opened with her going to live with Dr. Leslie after her grandmother's death, we should know as much about Anna as the book in its present form tells us.

The development of the relationship between the doctor and his ward, as she accompanies him on his calls and learns all he can teach her, inspired by Miss Jewett's own experiences with her father, is the finest part of the book. Anna's decision to become a doctor is accompanied by some lectures from the author on the role of women in the professions which impede the flow of the narrative, but the pace is picked up again when Anna goes to visit her aunt, Miss Prince, the first of Miss Jewett's flawless gallery of aristocratic old maids. There she becomes mildly involved with George Gerry. A delightful chapter describes a picnic where Anna and George happen upon a farmer who has hurt his shoulder and Anna, with one quick practiced pull, yanks the bone back into its socket. George, who has

Victorian ideas about the role of women, is understandably non-plused, yet he persists in his suit, and Anna at last must choose between him and her calling. It is a bit flat that she has so little difficulty deciding for the latter. Anna's resoluteness, her fine, early dedication of herself to a difficult profession, is one of her most attractive characteristics, but unfortunately it destroys all suspense in the book. Miss Jewett admitted that she was being a propagandist as well as a novelist; she deliberately interlarded the conversation of her characters with ideas that have more relevance to her philosophy than to her plot. In a long discussion between Dr. Leslie and his friend Dr. Ferris about the practice of medicine, the latter says: "I am in such a hurry to know what the next world is like that I can hardly wait to get to it." Miss Jewett, writing shortly after publication about the mysterious "step" of death just taken by General Grant, comments: "How one longs to take it for one's self!"

The disjointedness of *A Country Doctor* is corrected in *A Marsh Island* (1885), a charming, concentrated, well-balanced little novel of rustic love in the haying season. Its theme is the visit of Dick Dale, a rich young dilettante with a mild gift for painting, to the farm of Israel Owen where he boards for the summer to absorb the rural atmosphere. Dale allows himself to fall gently in love with the landlord's daughter, Doris Owen, temporarily disrupting her romance with Dan Lester, the village blacksmith. Doris does not fully comprehend what either man means to her: she exaggerates both her attraction to Dale and her irritation with Dan. When, on the outs with the latter and left alone by her parents on a hot, heavy, sleepy summer day, she goes listlessly for a walk on which we know her path will cross the painter's, the atmosphere becomes as suddenly ominous as in a George Eliot novel. Is it possible that she will be ruined as Hetty was ruined in *Adam Bede*? The ticking of the clock is made to sound like a warning. We rub our eyes. But no, of course not, we are in Miss Jewett's Maine where no such thing can happen, and Doris, escaping from her meeting undefiled and hearing that Dan, in despair, is shipping off to sea, hurries at dawn across the marshes to stop him — and catches him just in time. It is all as it should be for the kind of story it is, but slightness of theme shows more in a novel than in a short story. Miss Jewett was never to be entirely happy in the conventional novel form.

The death of her father in 1878 was a terrible blow and intensified her reluctance to take her place in a world of adults. Her friend Annie Fields pointed out that she was a curious combination of the immature and the advanced. "She never put her doll away and always used her child-names, but her plans were large and sometimes startling to others." One recognizes in this the traditional New England old maid. Three years after her father's death Miss Jewett was writing about him with the same kind of loving whimsicality that one finds in the letters of Emily Dickinson: "Today is father's birthday. I wonder if people keep the day they die for another birthday after they get to heaven? I have been thinking about him a very great deal this last day or two. I wonder if I am doing at all the things he wishes I would do, and I hope he does not get tired of me."

The great place that Dr. Jewett occupied in her mind and heart was ultimately filled by Annie Fields. Miss Jewett first met her through her husband, James T. Fields, the famous editor of the *Atlantic*. Annie Fields was a brilliant and charming woman, with a great gift for friendship, who presided over the most famous of Boston's literary salons on Charles Street. After her much older husband's death she traveled in Europe for a year with Miss Jewett, and thereafter, for the rest of the latter's life, they were constant companions or correspondents. Miss Jewett spent part of each winter in the Charles Street house and became almost as much a citizen of Boston as she was of Berwick.

Her horizon had never been provincial, but with her association with Annie Fields it became world-wide. As F. O. Matthiessen put it: "They ranged from Norway to Rome, and called on every one." They visited Christina Rossetti and stayed with the Arnolds, and, most excitingly of all, paid their respects to Lord Tennyson on the Isle of Wight. Miss Jewett was rapt: "No two men I have ever seen came up to Grant and Tennyson in GREATNESS." They called on Henry James. They went to Haworth Parsonage where three other women novelists had recorded the very soul of their countryside. Miss Jewett observed: "Nothing you ever read about them can make you know them until you go there. I can see the little pale faces of those sisters at the vicarage windows; and the Black Bull Inn, where the strange young brother used to comfort himself with light and laughter and country revelry, and break their hearts at the same time, is a little way down the hill. Never mind people who tell you there is nothing to see in the place where people lived who interest you. You always find something of what made them the souls they were, and at any rate you see their sky and their earth."

"You must know the world," she told Willa Cather, "before you can know the village."

In Berwick she had always loved to explore deserted houses, and in the south of France we find her pursuing the same enthusiasm. This might be the description of an impressionist canvas, a Pissarro or a Sisley: "And we went walking on, and presently we came to great gates, and still walked on with innocent hearts and a love of pleasure, and we crossed a moat full of flowers and green bushes, and the other side of the old bridge, beyond two slender marble columns with exquisite capitals, was another gateway and a court-yard and an old château asleep in the sun. All the great windows and the hall door at the top of the steps were open, and round the three sides and up to the top of the tower green vines had grown, with room enough to keep themselves separate, and one of them near by was full of bees, and you could hear no other sound. It was La Belle au Bois dormante. You just kept as still as you could and looked a little while, and came away again. And the stone of the château was reddish, and the green was green, and the sunshine was of that afternoon softness that made the whole sight of the old house flicker and smile back at you as if you were trying hard to look at something in a dream. It was in a lovely corner of the world, far out from any town."

The decade from 1886 to 1896 Miss Jewett devoted to the short story, producing five collections: *A White Heron and Other Stories* (1886); *The King of Folly Island and Other People* (1888); *Strangers and Wayfarers* (1890); *A Native of Winby and Other Tales* (1893); and *The Life of Nancy* (1895). These include all of her memorable fiction except *The Country of the Pointed Firs*.

The stories, almost without exception, succeed in direct proportion to their proximity to Miss Jewett's home base. "The Mistress of Sydenham Plantation" and "A War Debt" deal sentimentally with the gallant old southern gentry, their heads high in defeat, their protective darkies still loyal. She should have left them to Ellen Glasgow who saw behind the romance. "Mère Pochette" is an excursion into Balzacian territory, with its graphic picture of an avaricious old French Canadian hoarder whose vanity and meanness destroy her daughter and son-in-law and almost destroy her granddaughter. But Miss Jewett lacked either the fortitude or the pessimism to carry through to a Balzacian ending. That the old woman should destroy Manon's lover's letters without telling her is right for the *Comédie humaine*, but what would Sainte-Beuve have said to the *couleur-de-rose* ending when the grandmother repents and seeks out the lover to bring him to the ailing Manon in the nick of time? It is as if Eugénie Grandet married her hero and lived happily ever after.

"The Luck of the Bogans," "Between Mass and Vespers," and "A Little Captive Maid," all dealing with Irish immigrants, are curious examples of Miss Jewett's inability to catch the flavor of simple people outside of one ethnic group. "A Business Man," "The Two Browns," "Jim's Little Woman," "Fame's Little Day," and "The Life of Nancy" are all concerned more with plot than with background. They are in the O. Henry tradition and lack substance.

Almost all the remaining stories in the five volumes, however, deal happily with New Englanders against New England backgrounds, and the best are among the best of American short stories. Miss Jewett is at her most triumphant with the proud, dutiful, aristocratic old maid in reduced circumstances. "A Village Shop" is worthy of Hawthorne. Old Miss Esther Jaffrey, the great lady of the village, to the dismay and awe of her fellow citizens, opens a shop in the family mansion to support her worthless bookworm of a brother, Leonard, who, much like George Eliot's Mr. Casaubon, can do nothing but read Greek and Hebrew texts without ever producing even a line of comment. "The Dulham Ladies" has the sharp clarity and pathos of Elizabeth Gaskell's characterizations. The Misses Dobin, who live in the legend of a long-departed family superiority, at last make public fools of themselves by buying false locks to cover their thinning hair. Their tracing of their family name, Dobin, to d'Aubigné is worthy of *Emma,* but some of the occasionally unpleasant spinster sharpness of Jane Austen is also seen in this sentence: "The Reverend Mr. Dobin was never very enlightening in his discourses, and was providentially stopped short by a stroke of paralysis in the middle of his clerical career."

Then there are all the wonderful old Maine village women, sitting up and gossiping as they watch the dead, traveling with old bundles and cats to visit relatives, making up feuds of a lifetime's duration, dividing the poorhouse into hierarchies like the outside world, housekeeping for single ministers and sometimes winning husbands (for romance is never dead among Miss Jewett's old women), trying to decide which of three husbands' graves will be decorated with the rose, receiving old lovers who have become famous in the outside world. Miss Jewett told Willa Cather once that "when an old house and an old woman came together in her brain with a click, she knew that a story was under way." The old women are her particular trademark, with their shrewdness and humor and plain common sense and dutifulness and, above all, their ability to look the world straight in the eye without being in the least impressed.

Finest of all these tales is the title story of *The King of Folly Island.* The "king" is a recluse who lives on a small island, having sworn to desert mankind because of his failure to get the post of mail carrier in his home village. He is a charming old boy who delights the discontented middle-aged tycoon bachelor from the big city who tells the story, but the latter notes that the withering virgin daughter, a willing sacrificial lamb, is the victim of her father's self-imposed oath. The "king" understands her plight and wishes that he could do something to help her, but with a sad combination of selfishness and naiveté he does not see how he can go back on his word. He even goes so far as to offer her as a wife to his visitor, like Juliana Bordereau in James's *The Aspern Papers.* It is a haunting little tale of human waste with a pathetic ending when the narrator-tycoon in his city office receives in the mail from the now dying daughter the crude little house of shells of her own fashioning that he had been polite enough to admire.

The story, except for the narrator, would have fitted well into Miss Jewett's masterpiece, *The Country of the Pointed Firs*, which indeed contains another tale of an island recluse. The fascination of the theme may have derived from Miss Jewett's suspicion that the recluse on the Maine coast was simply a logical extension of the remoteness from the world of so many of the villagers whom she met. "The King of Folly Island" strikes again the note that was sounded in an early story, "A Lost Lover," the note of what, after all, so very great has been given up? *Had* one stayed in the busy world, had one wed the lover, would one have been so much better off? If the real life is the inner life, can any existence be so narrow as to rob a human being of the richness he has the determination to seek out?

Yet in "The Landscape Chamber," almost a ghost story, in which the young narrator happens upon a decayed mansion where an old miser and his daughter live, there is no question that Miss Jewett finds the human waste appalling. But there the vice of the miser is the kind that destroys all happiness, even in solitude. He is not a happy innocent, a simple-minded philosopher; he is a forlorn lunatic. The perfection of solitude is in the proper relation of oneself to natural things, like the little girl and the bird in that exquisite tale "A White Heron."

With *The Country of the Pointed Firs* (1896), near the end of her writing life, Miss Jewett returned to the fine straight highway of her first book but now with all the experience of twenty rich years of observing and recording. The novel of the Maine village, the string of loosely connected tales of characters in the same locale, was what she did best; indeed, it is her claim to enduring fame. When Ruth Draper, the monologist, asked Henry James if she would not do better to appear in a play, he replied: "My dear child, you have woven your own very beautiful little Persian carpet. Stand on it!" There are moments in Miss Jewett's fiction, particularly in her stories of the Irish, when one wishes that the master had given her the same advice. The device of Dunnet, the village in *The Country of the Pointed Firs*, has even the advantage that it can be added to.

Two of the best of her stories, "The Queen's Twin" and "A Dunnet Shepherdess," were written as sequels.

The narrator of the novel, never named but a lady writer of middle years, presumably single, comes to spend the summer in the coastal village of Dunnet, where she boards with Almira Todd, a widowed herb grower who supplements the work of the local doctor. For fifty cents a week the narrator rents the empty schoolhouse in which to do her writing, but her attention and soon her heart are quickly absorbed by the villagers. Mrs. Todd takes her about to meet everybody and fills in any missing backgrounds with stories. Captain Littlepage, cozily crazy, gives her an eerie account of the wraith-like creatures who live in the North Pole. She visits Shell-heap Island where "poor Joanna Todd," crossed in love, has died a recluse and hears her story; she attends the great reunion of the Bowden clan, a huge family picnic that includes everybody, for nearly everybody is kin. This is the special ceremony of the summer, a kind of genteel fertility rite. She goes out to Green Island to meet Mrs. Todd's wonderful, spry octogenarian mother, Mrs. Blackett, adored of the neighborhood, and her bachelor brother, William, whose forty-year courtship of Esther Hight, the mature "Dunnet shepherdess," culminates in marriage and makes a fitting ending for the book. And finally she meets Mrs. Martin, the "Queen's twin," who has been born on the same day as Queen Victoria and who has given her children the names of the princes and princesses. Her little cottage is filled with newspaper and magazine pictures of the glorious reign. The narrator keeps relating the village to its Anglo-Saxon origins and to its greater past in whaling and clipper ship days. The whole picture of Dunnet is charged with emotion, but very little of it can be expressed. A New England reserve covers all. When our guide takes her leave of Mrs. Todd in the end, she cannot quite bear it, feeling that some demonstration is at last called for, but she is firmly checked: "I could not part so; I ran after her to say good-by, but she shook her head and waved her hand without looking back when she heard my hurrying steps, and so went away down the street."

Isn't it too much? Are there not moments when these quaint lovable little women and men seem like figures in a Kate Greenaway sketch, or even like the bunny rabbits of Beatrix Potter? Never quite. That is Miss Jewett's secret. Dunnet may be seen too idyllically, if realism is what one wants, but this is not because the individuals are Greenaway ladies or bunny rabbits, but because they have been selected to substantiate the author's thesis that Dunnet is a lovely place, full of integrity, good neighborliness, thrift, and industry, as neat as it is honest, as tactful as it is unaffected, as simple as it is profound. No doubt she could have chosen types to illustrate the contrary; Miss Jewett was too much a doctor's daughter not to have heard about degeneracy in small, isolated New England communities. But what she chose to depict was the charm of the coastal village, and that such charm exists every visitor can testify. No other author has begun to catch it as she did, and it is unlikely now, with Maine drawn more and more into chain-store and television civilization, that there will be much of it left to catch in the future.

The Queen's Twin (1899) opens with two stories later included in editions of *The Country of the Pointed Firs*. With these exceptions the collection manifests a distressing increase of sentimentality, as if Miss Jewett's literary powers had become limited in later life to the depiction of Dunnet and that alone. "Where's Nora?" is the story of an Irish immigrant girl, dripping sweetness and light, who makes her fortune running a railway counter and returns happily to her native land. "Martha's Lady" is a vignette of the old-maid servant of an old maid who exists for forty years on the cherished memory of a few smiles and kindnesses meted out by her mistress' visiting niece. And "The Night before Thanksgiving" is the ultimate plunge into bathos: the rich young man who has made his fortune in the West returns in the nick of time to save his old foster mother from the poorhouse and give her a real Thanksgiving. Miss Jewett had come a long way from *Madame Bovary*.

She received a degree of Doctor of Literature from Bowdoin College in 1901, the year of publication for *The Tory Lover*. It is a pity that she did not receive it at the publication of *The Country of the Pointed Firs*, for *The Tory Lover* is her least distinguished book, the old maid at her most palpitating without the anchor of daily life.

Retreating into Berwick's past and the American Revolution, she populated her book with actual persons: John Paul Jones who sails from Berwick on the *Ranger*, Roger Wallingford, the reluctant patriot with British sympathies who becomes his most trusted officer, and the beautiful Mary Hamilton, Berwick's first heiress whom they both love. As in so many historical novels, everyone seems to know everyone else. The old Berwick schoolteacher turns out to be a peer who has changed his name and who as a youth in France knew both Fénelon and Voltaire. The hero meets Franklin and Philippe Égalité. Geography changes as rapidly as celebrities to meet the requirements of the cloak and dagger plot. All three of the principals meet in the end in a tavern in England: Wallingford having escaped from a British war prison, Mary having accompanied his mother, an unreconstructed Tory, back to the old country, and Jones, having slipped ashore from the *Ranger* in disguise. A Verdi librettist could hardly have equaled it.

In the early part of the book there are some beautiful descriptions of the elegant life of the rich Berwick shippers, whose big, white, slave-filled mansions recall the antebellum South, but the antiquing of the dialogue (every sentence has to begin with " 'Tis") makes it tiresome reading. Jones himself, as a man of violent, half-crazy tempers and fierce idealism, is totally beyond Miss Jewett's capacity and emerges as a sort of spinster's Ahab. The novel could be read with interest today only by a person seeking a picture of life in a prosperous New England coastal town of the eighteenth century. For if there was one thing Miss Jewett knew completely, it was the history of Berwick.

There were no more books after *The Tory Lover*. A carriage accident so damaged her nerves and balance that she had to give up creative writing in the last seven years of her life. She remained, however, alive and alert to all that was going on around her. Despite her famous letter of advice to Willa Cather in which she commented that the writer's lot is to "work in silence and with all one's heart," she had never been herself the kind of dedicated artist who lives only to write. Her writing had been a supplementation of her other interests. She wrote *Deephaven* "to make people of Maine better acquainted" and *A Country Doctor* to clear up some misconceptions about the medical profession. And one wonders if she did not have as much pleasure talking to her old women in their "best parlors" as she did in writing about them.

As she grew older she saw with regret that her subject matter was disappearing and turned to Jane Austen with all the old delight and a new sense of kinship. She wrote of *Persuasion*: "Dear me, how like her people are to the people we knew years ago! It is just as much New England before the war [Civil War] — that is, in provincial towns — as it ever was Old England."

And her glimpses of the new rich at play prompted this reaction: "The trouble is to us old-fashioned New Englanders that 'the cheap streak' so often spoils what there is of good inheritance, and the wrong side of our great material prosperity is seen almost everywhere. These are sad reflections!"

The end came with a sudden stroke in 1909, at the age of fifty-nine.

Willa Cather, who knew and deeply admired Miss Jewett in the last year of her life and to whom, in view of the tone of their letters, it is not straining a phrase to say that the torch was passed, describes the miracle of Miss Jewett's writing in her having caught the look, the look *itself*, that shines out at one from good country faces on remote farms. "To have got it down upon the printed page is like bringing the tenderest of early spring flowers from the deep wood into the hot light of noon without bruising its petals." And Henry James beautifully apologized for his critical neglect of Miss Jewett in his essay on Mr. and Mrs. Fields: "To speak in a mere parenthesis of Miss Jewett, mistress of an art of fiction all her own, even though of a minor compass, and surpassed only by Hawthorne as producer of the most finished and penetrating of the numerous 'short stories' that have the domestic life of New England for their general and their doubtless somewhat lean subject, is to do myself, I feel, the violence of suppressing a chapter of appreciation that I should long since somewhere have found space for. Her admirable gift, that artistic sensibility in her which rivaled the rare personal, that sense for the finest kind of truthful rendering, the sober and tender note, the temperately touched, whether in the ironic or the pathetic, would have deserved some more pointed commemoration than I judge her beautiful little quantum of achievement, her free and high, yet all so generously subdued character, a sort of elegance of humility or fine flame of modesty, with her remarkably distinguished outward stamp, to have called forth before the premature and overdarkened close of her young course of production."

2

EDITH WHARTON

IT WAS THE FASHION among Edith Wharton's friends, initiated by Henry James, to describe her in terms of glowing hyperbole, to see her in the guise of a great golden eagle swooping down from her high built palace of adventure to stir up the poor old croaking barnyard fowls. The woman is almost lost sight of in their boasts of her activities and possessions: the lovingly clipped and tended gardens, the gleaming, perfectly appointed interiors, the big, fast motor (purchased with the proceeds of the current book) bearing its multilingual owner and her faithful band over the roads of Europe to seek out in every nook and cranny the beauty that must redeem a modern wasteland. One imagines rooms refurbished and gardens relandscaped, all over Europe and the American East Coast, to conform with the mandates which she laid down in *The Decoration of Houses* and *Italian Villas and Their Gardens*. Indeed, there are moments when the lady whom Percy Lubbock describes in her Paris garden, fresh and trim, basket on arm, clippers in hand, ready for the daily task of shearing the heads of yesterday's roses, seems but the symbol of a larger self dedicated to sprucing up our very planet.

This is a long way from the picture in the minds of some American critics of a precious and snobbish old lady. Yet one can see how both pictures came into being. Perfection irritates as well as it attracts, in fiction as in life. As some of Mrs. Wharton's acquaintances complained that her taste in furnishing was too good, her French too precisely idiomatic, so have some of her critics found her heroes and heroines too exquisite, too apt to exclaim in rapt unison over little known beauties in art and literature with which the majority of her readers may not be equally familiar. The glittering structure of her cultivation sits on her novels like a rather showy icing that detracts from the cake beneath. That same majority may be put off by descriptions, however vivid, of physical objects and backgrounds that obtrude on the action, by being made to notice, even in scenes of tensest drama, a bit of red damask on a wall, a Jacqueminot rose, a small, dark Italian primitive. As Edmund Wilson points out, Mrs. Wharton was not only the pioneer but the poet of interior decoration.

Such cultivation was certainly not typical of her generation. Ladies of the New York and Newport of her day, educated by tutors, may have acquired a sound basis in German, French, and Italian, but they used these languages, if at all, more for dinner parties than for books. They did not spend their spare time, like Edith Newbold Jones, in their father's library, nor did they publish, at the age of sixteen, privately printed volumes of poetry. In fact, the very rarity of such intellectual achievement in the family of George Frederic Jones has lent comfort to the bearers of an old legend, totally without foundation, that Edith was the daughter of her brothers' English tutor, a clever young man with a mild painter's talent who was killed in the West by Indians. The theory seems to spring from the same kind of thinking that cannot conceive a Shakespeare born in Stratford. But I find it easier to believe that Lucretia Stevens Rhinelander Jones, granddaughter of a revolutionary patriot and a conventional society matron in a then small-town New York, should have had a brilliant daughter rather than an illegitimate one, and the fact that Edith, being so much younger than her brothers, was brought up like an only child seems adequate explanation for the hours that she spent alone in her father's library in West 23rd Street.

In her memoirs she describes as her good fortune that she was forbidden, on moral grounds, to read the ephemeral rubbish of the day and so was not distracted from the classics on the paternal shelves. It was obvious, she tells us, though I am not sure how quickly we agree, that a little girl "to whom the Old Testament, the Apocalypse and the Elizabethan dramatists were open, could not long pine for Whyte Melville or even Rhoda Broughton." In the sternly impressive list of her early reading, with its heavy emphasis on history and poetry, the only American names are Prescott, Parkman, Longfellow, and Irving. The other Melville, Herman, "a cousin of the Van Rensselaers, and qualified by birth to figure in the best society," she never, as a girl, even heard mentioned. Culture and education, to the Joneses and to their group, still meant Europe.

Europe, however, was not only the fountain of arts; it was also good for one's health and pocketbook. The Joneses were badly hit by the inflation that followed the Civil War and took their little daughter for long, economizing visits to Italy and France. It was a life of hotels and watering places, seeing only fellow Americans and their servants, but there were compensations for a sensitive child in driving out to the Campagna and wandering among the tombs of the Appian Way, in collecting fragments of porphyry and lapis lazuli on the slopes of the Palatine, and in such Parisian sights as the Empress Eugénie in her *daumont*, with the little Prince Imperial at her side and a glittering escort of officers. At the same time the young Henry James was knocking about the Continent, staying in pensions and picking up material for his first international tales. On both, the European experience was to have a lasting effect. But what was to have a much greater influence on Edith Jones as a writer, and to supply her with the subject material for her most important work, was neither her father's library nor her early impression of Europe, but her own clear, direct, comprehensive little girl's vision of the New York society in which her parents lived.

In 1862, the year of her birth, and for perhaps two decades thereafter, this was a small, sober, proper, tightly knit society, of Dutch and English descent, which lived in uniform streets of chocolate house fronts on income largely derived from municipal real estate. It was wary of the arts, beyond a dip into Longfellow or Bryant, or an evening of *Norma* at the Academy of Music, and disdainful of politics and any business that smacked of retail. The men practiced law in a listless sort of way and sat on charitable boards and had the leisure and taste to appreciate with their wives long meals of good food washed down by the "Jones Claret" or the "Newbold Madeira." Young Edith, sharply aware of their indifference to beauty in the arts, found their society stifling and stultifying, but as an elderly woman, surrounded by a world that seemed to her to have lost its values, she decided ruefully that the merit of those "amiable persons" had been to uphold standards of education and good manners and of scrupulous probity in business and private affairs.

As a young girl and as a debutante, she was miserably shy, a quality that was to dog her all her life, and that she was later to encase behind the enamel of formality, but by the time of her marriage, at the age of twenty-three, she had become at least outwardly reconciled to the observances of social life. Edward Robbins Wharton was an easygoing, friendly Bostonian, of no intellectual pretensions, who adored his much younger wife and always kept a thousand dollar bill in his purse in case "Pussy" wanted anything. They lived in New York and Newport and went every year to Europe, and no children came to interrupt their social and sightseeing routine. Obviously, it was not an existence to satisfy indefinitely a mind rendered immune to Rhoda Broughton by the beauties of the Apocalypse, and gradually the young wife started to write, here and there a poem, then a sentimental short story with an uplifting conclusion, then a a serious book on interior decoration, then travel pieces, at last a historical novel. In her memoirs she describes her writing as the natural sequence of a childhood habit of "making up" on bits of brown wrapping paper, but Edmund Wilson suggests that she took it up because of the tensions of an incompatible marriage and at the advice of Dr. S. Weir Mitchell, an early pioneer in female neuroses and himself a novelist. Fragments of her diary, recently published by Wayne Andrews, in which she notes that she could endure the "moral solitude" of her marriage only by creating a world of her imagination, certainly seem to substantiate Wilson. At any rate, there was the gap of a generation between those brown paper scribblings and the publication of her first volume of fiction at the age of thirty-seven.

The tales in *The Greater Inclination* (1899) and in its successor, *Crucial Instances* (1901), have some of the flavor of James's stories of artists and writers of the same period. They are apt to be set against European backgrounds and to deal with such themes as the temptation to the serious artist of commercial success or the bewildering influence upon him of the art of an older, richer civilization. They are clever and readable, if a trifle thin, and in three of them, "The Pelican," "The Rembrandt," and "The Angel at the Grave," Mrs. Wharton shows herself already in full command of the style that was to make her prose as lucid and polished as any in American fiction. It is a firm, crisp, smooth, direct, easily flowing style, the perfect instrument of a clear, undazzled eye, an analytic mind, and a sense of humor alert to the least pretentiousness. We may later wonder if her style was adapted to all the uses to which she put it, but at this point it perfectly presents to us, in all their pathetic and confused dignity, the brave little lady who lectures with an ignorant boldness to women's groups on every aspect of arts and letters, first for the love of her baby and ultimately for the love of her own voice, the proud and splendid widow who is induced only by direst poverty to part with her false Rembrandt, and the dedicated spinster who devotes a lifetime to maintaining her grandfather's house as a shrine for a public that has forgotten him. The defect in Edith Wharton's poetry, of which she published three volumes, is that this same style, consciously ennobled and stripped of laughter, becomes as dull and over-ornamented as the privately printed verse of any number of aspiring ladies who sought refuge from the distraction of social life. But poetry is subjective, and Mrs. Wharton, like many persons of wide reading and disciplined exterior, was inclined to be mawkish in subjective mood.

Her first novel, *The Valley of Decision,* appeared in 1902, when she was forty, and its scene is laid in Italy, that charnel house of English and American historical fiction. It is Edith Wharton's *Romola*, except that it is a better book than George Eliot's, for the fruits of her research are strewn attractively through the pages and not spooned into the reader like medicine. But although she captures remarkably the spirit and color of the eighteenth century, nothing can save the novel from its pale and lifeless characters. It is like a play with perfect settings in which the actors stand stiffly in the middle of the stage, their eyes fixed on the prompter. Only when Odo as a boy visits his grandfather's castle in the mountains, and later in the grand ducal gallery when he faces the portraits of his interbred ancestors, is there any true linking of characters and sets. The theme, however, is of some interest to the student of Edith Wharton, for it presages the political and social conservatism that was later to enchain her. Odo brings reform to Pianura only to find himself the harbinger and later the prisoner of the Reign of Terror. His creator was always afraid that even a needed cleaning of sewers might cause the collapse of the civilization above them.

The next two years find Mrs. Wharton still experimenting. *Sanctuary* (1903) demonstrates, a bit comically, the combined influence of Paul Bourget and James. In the first part of this absurd but charming little tale Kate Peyton marries a cheat and a liar in order to become the mother of the moral defective whom he might otherwise sire upon a woman less capable of raising such offspring — surely almost a parody of a Bourget theme — and in the second, twenty-five years later, she contrives to keep this offspring from committing an odious fraud by radiating sympathy to him in silent Jamesian waves. *The Descent of Man* (1904) is another volume of short stories, similar in tone to the earlier ones except for "The Dilettante," which marks an advance in the development of a male character who is to pervade all of Mrs. Wharton's fiction, the cold, cultivated, aristocratic egoist who feeds on the life and enthusiasm of simpler souls. The story has a clever twist at the end when the dilettante's betrothed jilts him on discovering that the lady who has been his intimate friend for years has *not* been his mistress. It is a theme that we shall meet again.

The House of Mirth (1905) marks her coming of age as a novelist. At last, and simultaneously, she had discovered both her medium and her subject matter. The first was the novel of manners and the latter the assault upon the old Knickerbocker society in which she had grown up of the new millionaires, the "invaders" as she called them, who had been so fabulously enriched by the business growth following the Civil War. New money had poured into New York in the 1880's and 1890's and turned the Joneses' quiet old Fifth Avenue into a dizzy parade of derivative façades from Azay-le-Rideau to the Porch of the Maidens. The Van Rensselaers and Rhinelanders might purse their lips at the ostentation of the Vanderbilts, but in a dollar world the biggest bank balance was bound to win out. A Livingston would marry a Mills, as in an earlier day a Schermerhorn had married an Astor. For what, really, did that older world have that was so special? It was all very well for James to describe the Newport of his childhood, surviving into this gilded age, as a little bare white open hand suddenly crammed with gold, but the fingers of that little hand closed firmly enough over the proffered bullion. The sober brown stucco of Upjohn's country villas concealed a materialism as rampant as any flaunted by the marble halls of Richard Morris Hunt. Mrs. Wharton saw clearly enough that the invaders and defenders were bound ultimately to bury their hatchet in a noisy, stamping dance, but she saw also the rich possibilities for satire in the contrasts afforded by the battle line in its last stages and the pathos of the individuals who were fated to be trampled under the feet of those boisterous truce makers.

Lily Bart, the heroine of *The House of Mirth*, stems from both worlds. Her father is related to the Penistons and the Stepneys, but is driven by her mother, a more ordinary creature, to make a fortune which, not being of invader blood, he is bound to lose. Lily, orphaned, is loosed on the social seas with only her beauty and charm for sails and no rudder but a ladylike disdain for shabby compromises and a vague sense that there must be somewhere a better life than the one into which she has drifted. Her rich friends, who use her as a social secretary to write notes and as a blind to shield them from importunate and suspicious husbands, cannot understand the squeamishness which keeps her, at the critical moment, from extracting a proposal from the rich bachelor whom she has not been too squeamish to pursue. Her respectable relatives, on the other hand, of an older society, cannot understand her smoking or gambling or being seen, however briefly, in the company of married men. Lily falls between two stools. She cannot bring herself to marry the vulgar Mr. Rosedale for all his millions, or the obscure Lawrence Selden, for all their affinity. She postpones decisions and hopes for the best and in the meanwhile seeks to distract herself. But we know from the start that she is doomed. She has only her loveliness, and what is that in a world that puts its store in coin and hypocrisy? The other characters, of both new and old New York, seem strangely and vindictively united in a constant readiness to humiliate her: Grace Stepney to tell tales on her, Mrs. Peniston to disinherit her, Bertha Dorset to abandon her in a foreign port, Gus Trenor to try to seduce her, his wife to say he has. We watch with agonized apprehension as Lily turns and doubles back, as she keeps miraculously rehabilitating herself, each time on a slightly lower level. For no matter how hard she struggles, without money she is unarmed in that arena. And in the end when she finally compromises and is willing to marry Rosedale, it is too late. He will not have her, and she falls to the job at the milliner's and the ultimate overdose of sleeping tablets. But we finish the book with the conviction that in the whole brawling, terrible city Lily is the one and only lady.

Of course, in sober afterthought it is incredible that supposed ladies and gentlemen should behave quite so despicably, that George Dorset should stand by so basely when his wife evicts Lily from the yacht, that Jack Stepney should be so grudging, that nobody should raise a finger to help Lily except Selden, who takes her to a hotel in a cab. But as one reads it, it is altogether convincing. The hunted creature is at bay; it is the whole brute world against, not the principles of Lily Bart, or even the good taste of Lily Bart, but simply, in the last analysis, against the beauty of Lily Bart. Lily's beauty is the light in which each of her different groups would like to shine, but when they find that it illuminates their ugliness they want to put it out. It is a beauty, however, that is indestructible, even in poverty, even in death, a beauty that the Trenors and Dorsets, with all their taste and money and ingenuity, can never hope to duplicate, a beauty that is the haunting symbol of what society might be — and isn't.

Lily's physical appearance gives a centripetal pull to a story that might otherwise ramble. When we first see her, through Selden's eyes in Grand Central Station, she is beginning to lose her purity of tint after eleven years of late hours and dancing, yet everything about her is still "vigorous and exquisite, at once strong and fine." Not until he sees her in her last great social triumph, as Reynolds' Mrs. Lloyd in a *tableau vivant* at the Brys', with poised foot and lifted arm, all "soaring grace," is the full poetry of her loveliness revealed to him. Then he sees her as divested of the trivialities of her world and catching "a note of that eternal harmony of which her beauty was a part."

As adversity deepens, he notices a subtle change in her appearance. It has lost the transparency through which fluctuations of the spirit were sometimes tragically visible and has fused into a hard, brilliant substance. Later, at the reading of Mrs. Peniston's disinheriting will, we see her "tall and noble in her black dress." Rosedale meets her in the street, drooping with lassitude, and is struck by the way the dark penciling of fatigue under her eyes and the morbid, blue-veined pallor of her temples bring out the brightness of her hair and lips. He sees her beauty as a "forgotten enemy" that has lain in ambush to spring out on him unawares. And Selden, watching her for the last time kneeling on the hearthrug, will remember long afterward "how the red play of the flame sharpened the depression of her nostrils, and intensified the blackness of the shadows which struck up from her cheekbones to her eyes." A few hours later he is to see her on her narrow bed, "with motionless hands and calm, unrecognizing face, the semblance of Lily Bart."

The different levels of society in *The House of Mirth* are explored with a precision comparable to that of Proust, whom Mrs. Wharton was later so greatly to admire. We follow Lily's gradual descent from "Bellomont" on the Hudson and the other great country houses of a world where the old and new societies had begun to merge, to the little court of the Gormers, who, although rich enough to be ultimately accepted, are still at the stage of having to fill their house with hangers-on, to the bogus intellectual world of Carry Fisher who pretends to like interesting people while she earns her living helping climbers up the social ladder, to the final drop into the gilded hotel of the demimondaine Norma Hatch. Lily learns that money is the common denominator of all these worlds and that the differences between them consist only in the degrees of scent with which its odor is from time to time concealed. Van Wyck Brooks accused Mrs. Wharton of knowing nothing of the American West, and perhaps she did not, but she had a firsthand knowledge of where the profits of the frontier had gone. Lily Bart, weary on foot, watching the carriages and motors of her former friends ply up and down Fifth Avenue, Mrs. Van Osburgh's C-spring barouche, Mrs. Hatch's electric victoria, is seeing the natural successors of the covered wagon.

I do not suppose that Mrs. Wharton intended Lawrence Selden to constitute the last and greatest of Lily's trials, but so he strikes me. He is a well-born, leisurely bachelor lawyer, with means just adequate for a life of elegant solitude, who spends his evenings, when not leafing through the pages of his first editions, dining out in a society that he loves to ridicule. Lily knows that he is a neutral in the battle of life and death in which she is so desperately engaged, and she asks only that he hold her hand briefly in moments of crisis or brush her lips with a light kiss. He does, in the end, decide to marry her, but as she has been too late for Rosedale, so is he too late for her, and he can only kneel by her bed and give to her lifeless lips the last of his airy kisses. Mrs. Wharton's attitude toward Selden's type of man is enigmatic. He may be a villain in "The Dilettante," or he may at least pose as a hero in *The House of Mirth*. She is careful in the latter to point out for his sake, whenever he condemns Lily Bart, that appearances have been against her. Perhaps she conceived him as an abused lover in the Shakespearean sense, as an Othello or a Posthumus. But Othello and Posthumus are quick to believe the worst because of the very violence of their passions. An eye as dry as Selden's should be slower to be deceived. I incline to the theory that Mrs. Wharton really intended us to accept this plastercast figure for a hero, but that she had a low opinion of heroes in general. When Lily suddenly retorts to Selden that he spends a great deal of his time in a society that he professes to despise, it is as if the author had suddenly slipped into the book to express a contempt that the reader is not meant to share.

The enigma of Selden inevitably leads to a consideration of the deepest friendship of Edith Wharton's life. "The year before my marriage," she relates in her memoirs, "I had made friends with a young man named Walter Berry, the son of an old friend of my family's (and indeed a distant cousin)." Despite the note of kinship thus cautiously sounded, there is a legend that he proposed to her and was turned down as a not good enough match. This might, if true, explain in the light of revenge some of his acts of coldness to her in later years. At any rate, he became a friend of the young Whartons, and it was during one of his visits to their house in Newport that she showed him the "lumpy pages" of an early manuscript and had the mortification of hearing his "shout of laughter," a peal that was never quite to cease ringing in her ears. But a minute later he said good-naturedly, "Come, let's see what can be done," and settled down beside her to try to model the lump into a book. In that modeling process she claimed, decades later, that she had been taught whatever she knew about the writing of "clear concise English."

I do not believe it, though I am sure that she did. There seemed no limits to her admiration of Berry. "He found me when my mind and soul were hungry and thirsty, and he fed them till our last hour together." Evidently, he supplied her with the intellectual and spiritual companionship that she had never found with Edward Wharton. The latter, as her writing and fame developed, had shrunk to a kind of cipher in her life. In her memoirs Consuelo Vanderbilt Balsan recalls him "as more of an equerry than an equal, walking behind her and carrying whatever paraphernalia she happened to discard." It was only to be expected, under the circumstances, that she should fall in love with Berry, yet it is not until 1908, when she was forty-six, that her journal begins to evidence it. "I should like to be to you, friend of my heart, like a touch of wings brushing by you in the darkness, or like the scent of an invisible garden that one passes by on an unknown road." The tone of this and other entries would seem to confirm the opinion of many of those close to her that she received only friendship in return. Berry, according to them, was perfectly willing to let her play her chosen role of the touch of wings or the invisible garden. But these, of course, had been only phrases. Like any woman, she wanted more: "You hurt me — you disillusioned me — and when you left me, I was more deeply yours." When he went to Cairo to be a judge of the International Tribunal, she could hardly endure it: "Oh, my adored, my own love, you who have given me the only moments of real life I have ever known, how am I to face the long hours and days?" But she did face them, and one wonders if correspondence with so tepid an admirer might not have been simpler in the end than talks and scenes.

What sort of man was he? James seems to have liked him and to have enjoyed their faintly catty old bachelors' correspondence in which Mrs. Wharton, because of her raids into the secluded re- treats of friends, is described as "the angel of devastation." But to others of her circle Berry was less sympathetic, and to Percy Lub- bock he was a dogmatic and snobbish egotist, the evil genius, in- deed, of her life. "None of her friends," he put it bluntly, "thought she was the better for the surrender of her fine free spirit to the con- trol of a man, I am ready to believe, of strong intelligence and abili- ty — but also, I certainly know, of a dry and narrow and supercilious temper."

Mrs. Wharton's attitude toward evasion of the marriage vow was always ambiguous. Divorce (though she was to come to it herself) she considered crude and antisocial, and the facile forming of new marital ties unspeakably vulgar. On the other hand, the dishonesties and evasions of concealed adultery struck her as offensive and de- grading, while any open disregard of the conventions led to a slow, sordid end in those shabby European watering places with which the minds of her contemporaries seemed always to identify extra- marital passion. Perhaps, finally, the latter course seemed best to her. At least the spirit that was capable of facing it seemed the finest spirit. Paulina Trant in "The Long Run" (included in *Xingu*, 1916) has all her creator's sympathy when she offers to give up her husband and home for love, and Halston Merrick, who logically and sensibly tries to reason her out of it, appears as the shallowest of lovers. There must have been womanly moments, for all of Edith Wharton's admiration of Berry, when he struck her as a bit of a Halston Mer- rick, when she saw him with eyes that made even Lubbock's seem charitable by comparison. It is perhaps to such moments that we owe the curious ambivalence in her treatment of heroes.

Despite the great critical and popular success of *The House of Mirth*, Mrs. Wharton did not return to her New York subject matter for another eight years. Perhaps she was afraid of exhausting it too quickly. *Madame de Treymes* and *The Fruit of the Tree*, so radically different from each other, both appeared in 1907. The first is a true Jamesian tale of innocents abroad, as subtle and fine as any of James's own but with more liveliness and humor. It portrays the duel between John Durham, an American hero in the tradition of James's Christopher Newman, and a wily, charming Parisian aristocrat, Madame de Treymes, over the latter's sister-in-law, poor little Fanny Frisbee of brownstone New York, who has found only misery in her French marriage. Principles and ideals, for the last time in Edith Wharton's fiction, are found on the side of the Stars and Stripes, and Madame de Treymes ruefully recognizes the moral superiority of the Yankee in her final sob: "Ah, you poor, good man!" In later years, unhappily, Mrs. Wharton's Americans abroad were to become the corrupters and not the corrupted.

The Fruit of the Tree is an experiment in a totally new field, the novel of reform. Mrs. Wharton began her task of research conscientiously enough with a tour of a factory near her country home in Lenox, Massachusetts, but she soon lost interest in her theme and succumbed to an unworthy compromise. In order to be able to draw her factory manager and trained nurse from models in her own world, she endowed them both with old and distinguished families which had only recently lost their money, thus giving to these parts of her book a curious air of social masquerade. Even so, the reader's interest is caught when Amherst, the priggish manager, marries the widow owner of the factory, having misconstrued her passion for himself as a zeal for the cause of the workers, and settles down in blithe ignorance to what he imagines will be their shared task of reform. But at this point Mrs. Wharton changes her theme altogether. Bessie Amherst, bored with the workers and interpreting, perhaps correctly (again the enigma of the Wharton hero), her husband's interest in reform as indifference to herself, goes galloping over icy roads until she falls from her horse and receives an incurable back injury, which condemns her to a long period of hideous and futile agony. The novel now turns abruptly into a problem novel about euthanasia in the manner of Bourget, for Bessie's sufferings are abbreviated by the needle of the trained nurse with the social background. Mrs. Wharton handles both themes competently, but the book simply collapses between them. The failure of *The Fruit of the Tree* is just the opposite of that of *The Valley of Decision*; the settings, and not the characters, fade away. It is, however, a less disastrous fault. Bessie Amherst, indolent, selfish, but quite ready to be led by any man who will take the trouble to understand her, is interesting enough to make the novel readable even today, when industrial reform of the type in question has long since been effected and when euthanasia, if still illegal, has ceased to be morally shocking.

The Hermit and the Wild Woman (1908) is another volume of slender, contrived Jamesian stories of artists and dilettantes, but *Tales of Men and Ghosts* (1910) contains some superb chillers. A tricky ending to a serious short story will sometimes detract from the total effect and make it seem superficial or sentimental, or both, but in a ghost story it has a valid, even an indispensable, function. The egotism of Mrs. Wharton's constantly recurring bachelors is brought out more effectively in "The Eyes" than in any of her other short stories or novels. Culwin tells a listening group about a fire, which includes his young protégé, of the eyes, the old eyes with sunk orbits and thick, red-lined lids and look of vicious security, that haunt him at night whenever he has performed what he deems an unselfish act, which the reader, of course, knows to have been just the opposite. As he finishes his tale he marks the horror on the features of the protégé, with whose youth and bloom he has tried to water his own dry nature, and turning to look in the mirror behind him, he sees at last whose eyes they are.

Mrs. Wharton's other ghost stories may be considered out of chronology because their style and effectiveness does not vary, except to improve, with the years. This kind of tale requires a skill that never left her, the skill of telling a story reduced to its bare bones, without the aid of social problems or manners or mores or even of human nature, except in its most elemental sense. She always believed that the storytelling faculty was basic in any writer. She was like a representational artist who looks askance at an abstract painting and wants to know if the man who executed it can really draw. At times she would try her hand, almost as one might try a puzzle, at a story that was nothing but technique, like "Roman Fever," where the interest and excitement are concentrated in the last line that gives the whole meaning to what has gone before. Her technique in ghost stories is to keep the supernatural to the minimum that will still irradiate the tale with horror. Character can be important as in "The Eyes," but it is by no means essential. As long as there is one plain human being, as in "All Souls," to register terror for the reader, there is an adequate cast.

Time, as we shall see, brought to Mrs. Wharton an attitude of disapproval toward the changing social scene which was to sour her later work, but the ghost stories, by their very nature, escaped this, and her grasp of the secret of chilling her reader continued to improve to the end. "The Lady's Maid's Bell," an early venture, suffers from a slight overdose of the eerie. There is not only the bell; there is the constantly reappearing ghost of Emma Saxon. "Pomegranate Seed," a later tale, corrects this. A second wife's happiness is destroyed and her life turned to nightmare by the appearance, at irregular intervals, on the hall table, addressed to her husband in a faint, female handwriting, of envelopes which unnerve him but which he refuses to discuss. The conviction that these missives come from the dead wife begins to dawn on the reader at the same time that it dawns on her successor, and in the mood of horror that we share with her we completely accept her husband's final disappearance. The ghost of the first wife never comes on the scene to derogate from her letters as Emma Saxon does from the bell.

In the compilation *Ghosts* (1937), published in the last year of Mrs. Wharton's life, two of the best of the eleven stories, "Miss Mary Pask" and "Bewitched," deal, not with the supernatural, but with the appearance of it. Here Mrs. Wharton sets herself the difficult task of scaring the reader in a ghost story without the aid of a ghost. The atmosphere has to be made correspondingly more omi-

nous; Mary Pask must be whiter and more wraithlike on that foggy
night in Brittany than if she were a true spirit, and the New Englanders of "Bewitched" must be gaunter and grimmer than the characters
of *Ethan Frome* to make sufficiently terrible the ending that proves
Venny Brand to have been masquerading. The last story of the collection, and its masterpiece, "A Bottle of Perrier," is not really a
ghost story at all, but a tale of hatred and murder in the African desert where an eccentric Englishman lives in a lonely castle with his
butler and a host of Arab servants. Mrs. Wharton's style is at its
richest as she sets her African scene: "The afternoon hung over the
place like a great velarium of cloth-of-gold stretched across the battlements and drooping down in ever slacker folds upon the heavy-
headed palms. When at length the gold turned to violet, and the west
to a bow of crystal clasping the dark sands, Medford shook off his
sleep and wandered out." And the final sentence which reveals for
the reader where the body of Almodham has all the time been rot-
ting is like one of those screaming chords at the end of Strauss's
Salome: "The moon, swinging high above the battlements, sent a
searching spear of light down into the guilty darkness of the well."

In 1911 Mrs. Wharton published the short novel with which her
name has ever since been linked and which sometimes threatens to
pre-empt the whole of her niche in the history of American literature.
She says in her memoirs that in writing *Ethan Frome* she felt for the
first time the artisan's full control of his implements. In later years
its continuing success was to plague her, as the success of "Daisy
Miller" plagued James, for she could never agree with the critics
who claimed that it was her best work. Yet it is surely among her
best. When I think of it, I visualize a small painting, perfectly executed to the last detail, of three silent figures in a small dark cottage
kitchen, with snow glimpsed through a window, the terrible Zeena
in the center, white and pasty and gaunt, and, scattered on the table,
the pieces of a broken dish. But I could never put the story as fiction
in the same class with *The House of Mirth* on the very ground that
to me it *is* a picture and, as such, one dimensional. Lily Bart and the
society in which she lives are turned around and around and studied
from different angles. It is not fair, of course, to compare a long

novel with a novelette, but the tremendous reputation of *Ethan Frome* evokes such a defense.

There has been some disposition in critics to view with distrust Mrs. Wharton's excursions into life among the needy, as evidenced by *Ethan Frome*, "The Bunner Sisters," and *Summer*, to see her as the great lady from "The Mount" in Lenox, peering at Ethan and his womenfolk from the back seat of her big motor. I doubt if these comments would have been made had the stories been published under another name, for the keenness of Mrs. Wharton's observation was not affected by the social status of her models. Only, in later years, when she attempted to describe persons and places that she had never seen did she fail in her job. I am totally persuaded of the reality of that notions shop kept by Ann Eliza Bunner and her sister and by the dank public library where Charity Royall dreams away her listless days. The reason why *Summer* and "The Bunner Sisters" are less convincing than *Ethan Frome* does not lie in any failure of observation or imagination on the part of the author, but in the fact that one feels her presence, which in *Ethan Frome* the device of a narrator has successfully eliminated. When Charity Royall sees her mother's kinfolk on the mountain "herded together in a sort of passive promiscuity in which their common misery was the strongest link," and when Evalina Bunner, contrasted to the Hochmullers, is described as "a faintly washed sketch beside a brilliant chromo," we see clearly enough what is meant, but we are standing on that mountain and at Evalina's wedding with Mrs. Wharton herself, and we feel with a touch of constraint the incongruity of our presence.

The Reef (1912) was greeted with a burst of congratulation from all the Jamesian circle. "Racinian" was the adjective used by the master, and indeed a Racinian unity of mood is achieved by centering the action in an old, high-roofed château of brick and yellowish stone, bathed in the pale light of October afternoons. The rooms in which the characters tensely talk are like a series of paintings by Walter Gay. It is a quiet, controlled, beautiful novel, but its theme has always struck me as faintly ridiculous. Mrs. Leath, a widow, is at last about to marry George Darrow, her old bachelor admirer, and her stepson, Owen, is entertaining a similar plan with respect to the beautiful young family governess, Sophy Viner, when the discovery that Darrow and Sophy have once been lovers reduces all the characters to a state of quiet desperation. Even conceding that in 1912 such an affair might have disqualified Sophy as a bride for Owen, would Mrs. Leath, a woman who had lived all her adult years in France, consider that her own happiness had to be sacrificed as well? Of course, Mrs. Wharton's answer would be that Mrs. Leath is a woman of the finest sensitivities and that the affair occurred at a time when she had every reason to believe Darrow attentive to herself, but I still cannot get away from the suspicion that at least part of the horror of the situation lies in the fact that Sophy is a governess. The final chapter, so jarringly out of tune with the rest of the book, tends to confirm this suspicion. When Mrs. Leath goes to Sophy's sister's hotel to tell Sophy that she has given Darrow up, she is received by the sister in a dim, untidy, scented room, complete with lover and masseur. Coarse and bloated as the sister is, Mrs. Leath can nonetheless see in her what the beautiful Sophy will one day become, and when she discovers that the latter has departed for India in the company of a disreputable woman, she takes her hasty leave, presumably to return to Darrow and happiness.

The only moral that I can make out of this is that Sophy Viner, a paid dependent who is an appendage rather than a true part of the social pattern, may be expected, under the first bad influence, to drop to a life of semi-prostitution. If the problem to which the book is addressed be justified as a problem common to the era, there remains to be justified the point of view of the author, which for once seems as narrowly prudish and class-conscious as her bitterest critics have ever accused it of being.

The Custom of the Country, happily, in the following year, 1913, is a return to the rich, sure ground of New York and the novel of manners, only this time the central character in the conflict of social groups is not a victim but an invader. Undine Spragg is a creature of alloy, as sentimental in her judgments of herself as she is ruthless in her judgments of others. A father is only a checkbook, a husband a means of social advancement, a baby a threat to the figure. No amount of association with cultivated persons or of exposure to the art of Europe can ripple the surface of her infinite vulgarity. She never knows the toll in human misery of her advance to the social heights, for it never occurs to her to look back. The story of how she hews her way through the old New York ranks of the Marvells and Dagonets, already weakened by prior compromises with the invaders, and even into the society of the Faubourg Saint-Germain from which James's "American" was barred, is vivid and fascinating. Undine gets into as many dangerous corners as Lily Bart, but by miscalculation rather than by inertia, and the same shrewd, restless cerebration that gets her in can be counted on to get her out. In *The House of Mirth* our compassion goes out to Lily; in *The Custom of the Country* it goes out to the society which Undine is trying to crash.

The flaw in the novel that keeps it from ranking equally with its predecessor is that Mrs. Wharton hates Undine too much. She sees in her incarnate the devil of the modern world, that world where all fineness of soul and graciousness of living have been submerged in a great tide of insipid and meretricious uniformity whose origin seems to lie vaguely in the American Middle West. New York has been lost to the flood, and even Europe is no longer safe. The family of the Marquis de Chelles are not sufficiently humiliated by his marriage to Undine; they must also see their tapestries stripped from their walls by her next husband, Elmer Moffatt. What would the wiles of even Madame de Treymes have accomplished against Elmer? James complained to Mrs. Wharton that she had not sufficiently developed the theme of the relationship between the Chelleses and Undine. Surely, he was wrong. Surely, as the book indicates, no such relationship could have even existed. What Mrs. Wharton fails to prove is that Chelles would have married Undine at all. For she is really too awful to be quite so successful with quite so many men. Her vulgarity destroys the allure that such a woman would have been bound to have and that her creator was not to understand until her last, unfinished novel.

Lily Bart takes only one trip to Europe in the course of her saga, but Undine spends half of hers there. It was abroad, indeed, that Mrs. Wharton must have observed her prototypes, for in these years she had been spending less and less time in her own country. She had always been attracted by the order and grace of French living and by the assured social position of intellectuals in France, so different from what she had experienced in New York. She had a deep respect for traditions and ceremonials that gave her some assurance that the existing form of society had a basis in the past, and, by a like token, a hope for preservation in the future. The New York of her younger years had had traditions, but she had found them merely restricting. The dead hand of a Manhattan past had seemed to her simply dead. Her writing, for example, had never been recognized by her friends and relations as anything but a vaguely embarrassing habit that was better not mentioned. Her husband, it was true, took a rather childish pride in her growing fame, but in all intellectual matters he was as bad as the others. "Does that sort of thing really amuse you?" he asked when she showed him a striking passage in R. H. Lock's study of heredity and variation. "That is the answer to everything worth-while!" she moaned in her journal. "Oh, Gods of derision! And you've given me twenty years of it! *Je n'en peux plus.*"

This cry of the heart is dated 1908 when she was forty-six. Release was on its way. In 1910 the Whartons sold the house in Lenox and moved permanently to France. In the same year Edward Wharton had a nervous collapse and was placed in a sanatorium. In 1913 they were divorced. She had found at last a world where everything blended: beautiful surroundings, intellectual companionship, a society that combined a respect for the past with a vital concern for the present. London was within easy reach, and she could be in constant touch with writers whose conversation was as polished and civilized as their prose: James, Bourget, Lubbock, Howard Sturgis. It is easy to comprehend the charm of such a life, but what did it have to do with the contemporary American scene that it was her profession to study? James in his later years built his characters into an exotic world of his own imagination. It was not necessary for the creator of Maggie Verver or Milly Theale to have an up-to-date knowledge of life on the other side of the Atlantic. It was enough that he had been born American. But Edith Wharton was concerned with representing the life and manners of New York, and for this she needed more than the chatter of tourist friends.

In a surprisingly insipid little book, *French Ways and Their Meaning* (1919), made up of articles originally written to acquaint Americans coming to France during the war with the character of their allies and hosts, Mrs. Wharton descants on the Gallic qualities of taste, reverence, continuity, and intellectual honesty. The picture that emerges, quite unintentionally, is of a nation chained to ancient forms and observances which could hardly have survived four years of trench warfare with the first military power of Europe. Mrs. Wharton was paying France what she deemed the greatest compliment she knew in describing as national virtues the qualities that most attracted her in her own polite, intellectual circle. There is some of the self-justification of the expatriate in the attitude that her adopted country had to possess to the fullest degree, and her native land to the least, the civilized atmosphere which she found so indispensable in daily life. As a result, there was always a presumption in favor of France in her thinking, just as there was one against America, an injustice that is everywhere reflected in this misleading little book. When she speaks of French culture, Richelieu and the Academy are invoked, but when it is a question of American, she cites only the middle-western college girl who "learnt art" in a year.

When crisis came, at any rate, she had proved a true, if not a legal, citizen of France. She scorned the expatriates who scuttled home at the first rumble of danger in the summer of 1914 and whom she later described in *The Marne*. She was passionately involved from the beginning with the land of her adoption and threw herself into work for the refugees and the wounded with a fervor and efficiency which resulted in her being decorated by President Poincaré and named an officer of the Legion of Honor. She regarded the war from a simple but consistent point of view: France, virtually single-handed, was fighting the battle of civilization against the powers of darkness. It was the spirit that made men fight and die, but it has never, unfortunately, been the spirit of fiction. Reading *The Marne* (1918) and *A Son at the Front* (1923) today gives one the feeling of taking an old enlistment poster out of an attic trunk. It may be a significant comment on the very nature of Armageddon that the only literature that survives it is literature of disillusionment and despair.

Mrs. Wharton knew that the war was terrible; she had visited hospitals and even the front itself. But the exhilaration of the noncombatant, no matter how dedicated and useful her services, has a shrill sound to postwar ears.

The corrosive effect of war on a civilization already vulgarized by American money induced in Mrs. Wharton a mood of nostalgia for the old quiet New York world of her childhood that she had once found so confining. Much later she was to write: "When I was young it used to seem to me that the group in which I grew up was like an empty vessel into which no new wine would ever again be poured. Now I see that one of its uses lay in preserving a few drops of an old vintage too rare to be savoured by a youthful palate."

There was no rose color, however, in the glasses through which she viewed the past. She did not flinch at sight of the old prejudices; she simply reinterpreted them. Mrs. Lidcote, in "Autre Temps" (*Xingu*) has been ostracized for leaving her husband for a lover, but when she returns to New York, a generation later, to take her stand by her daughter who has done the same thing, she discovers that times have changed and that her daughter can now marry her lover and be received by the very people who have cut Mrs. Lidcote. The times, however, have changed only for the daughter's generation. Society will not revise its judgments of individuals, and Mrs. Lidcote must dine upstairs on a tray in order not to embarrass a dinner party gathered to beam on the young lovers. But there is another, subtler moral in the story, and that is in the suggestion that Mrs. Lidcote, with all her suffering, has had a richer life than her daughter with her easy divorce and remarriage. She may feel like a lonely anachronism as she returns to her exile in Europe, but there is no envy in her reflections: "Where indeed in this crowded, topsy-turvey world, with its headlong changes and helter-skelter readjustments, its new tolerances and indifferences and accommodations, was there room for a character fashioned by slower sterner processes and a life broken under their inexorable pressure?"

But this is nostalgia for the very brand that did the burning! Ten years later, in *Twilight Sleep*, Mrs. Wharton was to go even further in her stand against the vapid painlessness of the postwar world by ridiculing the heavy doping of mothers in childbirth. The past came to have a certain validity to her simply by being the past. The New York of her childhood, that "cramped horizontal gridiron of a town without towers, porticoes, fountains or perspectives, hide-bound in its deadly uniformity of mean ugliness," having vanished, became as fascinating as Atlantis or Troy. It is to this attitude of apology toward her parents' generation that we owe her finest novel.

The title, *The Age of Innocence*, refers to the New York of the 1870's in the girlhood of Edith Jones and gives to the book the flavor of a historical novel, as is often pointed out by critics. The fact not always recognized by critics is that it was a habit of Victorian novelists to set their stories in the era of their childhood. The novelist of manners has since shown a tendency to revert to a usually recent past where social distinctions, which make up so much of his subject matter, were more sharply defined, or at least where he thinks they were. *The Age of Innocence* (1920) is written in a Proustian mood of remembered things that evokes the airless atmosphere of an old, ordered, small-town New York as vividly as a conversation piece by Eastman Johnson. Here the dilettante bachelor, Newland Archer, as usual a lawyer, is at last placed in a story adapted to bring out the best and the worst in him. For he must have enough passion and imagination to aspire to break through the barriers of convention that surround him and yet be weak enough so that he cannot finally escape the steely embrace of an aroused tribe. Newland knows that he never really has a chance from the beginning; that is his pathos. He is engaged to May Welland, and he will marry May Welland and spend a lifetime with May Welland, and that is that, and both he and May's beautiful, Europeanized, disenchanted cousin, Ellen Olenska, realize it and accept it.

But against the smallness and vapidity of its inhabitants the physical background of New York and Newport is painted with a richness of color and detail that delights the imagination. It is this constant contrast that makes the uniqueness of the novel. The old Academy of Music, with its shabby red and gold boxes, its carefully brushed, white-waistcoated, buttonhole-flowered gentlemen; the Julius Beauforts' conservatory, where camellias and tree ferns arch their foliage over seats of black and gold bamboo; May Archer's living room, with its little plush tables covered with silver toys and efflorescent photograph frames; the small bright lawns and big bright sea of Newport — these scenes succeed each other like colored slides.

We have a suffocating sense of a creature trapped and doomed as poor Newland comes to the awareness, from the exchanged glances, coughs, and silences that surround him, that all of his vast family and family-in-law, including his own wife, are convinced that he is enjoying the very affair that he has failed to achieve and are united in irresistible tact to cut it short. But Mrs. Wharton is not suggesting that Newland and Ellen, in their renunciation of each other, have condemned themselves to a life of unrewarding frustration. Rules and regulations have now their validity to her, no matter what passions they crush. "It was you," Ellen tells Archer, "who made me understand that under the dullness there are things so fine and sensitive and delicate that even those I most cared for in my other life look cheap in comparison." And a generation later Archer sees no cause to repine in thinking back over his married life with May: "Their long years together had shown him that it did not so much matter if marriage was a dull duty, as long as it kept the dignity of a duty: lapsing from that, it became a mere battle of ugly appetites. Looking about him, he honored his own past, and mourned for it. After all, there was good in the old ways."

It is Edith Wharton's tribute to her own background, this affirmation that under the thick, smoky glass of convention bloom the fine, fragile flowers of patient suffering and self-sacrifice. To run away from society may be as vulgar in the end as to crash it. Newland Archer builds a shrine in his heart around the image of Ellen from which he derives strength to endure his uneventful and moderately useful life, a life where civic and social duties are judiciously balanced and where the impetus of Theodore Roosevelt even gets him into the state legislature, if only for a single term. We see him more completely than any other of Mrs. Wharton's heroes, and the reader who doubts that such a type existed has only to turn the pages of the voluminous diary of George Templeton Strong, published long after Edith Wharton's death.

The comparison with Strong's diary is also relevant in that *The Age of Innocence* is the first of Mrs. Wharton's novels to have all the action seen through the eyes of one character. The interest is thus centered in Newland Archer, as the interest in the two later books where she used the same method, *The Mother's Recompense* and *The Children*, is centered in Kate Clephane and Martin Boyne. Unlike James, however, she refused to be limited in her own comments to her central character's point of view. Archer's conventional way of looking at life, at least in the first half of the book, is too dull a lens for the reader, and his creator never hesitates to peer over his shoulder and point out all kinds of interesting things on the New York scene that we would otherwise miss. James would have objected to this. He would have argued that the spiritual growth of Archer, like that of Lambert Strether in *The Ambassadors*, would have a richer significance if viewed entirely through Archer's mind. It was one of their principal points of division. Mrs. Wharton refused to subordinate to any rule of design the "irregular and irrelevant movements of life" that to her made up the background of her stories.

It is interesting that her name should be so constantly linked with James's, considering how different were their approaches to their art. His influence is visible, superficially, in her early work, and, of course, they were both interested in Americans in Europe, but there the resemblance ceases. James was subtle, speculative, and indirect; Edith Wharton was always clear and to the point. Percy Lubbock speaks of her aversion to the abstract, to any discussion of the conundrum of life's meaning. She dealt with definite psychological and social problems and handled them in her own definite way. Her sentences never have to be read and reread, like James's, for richer and deeper disclosures. Furthermore, she and James, although good friends, never appreciated the best in each other's work. He found her most successful when most under his influence, as, for example, in *The Reef*, while she distrusted the whole artistic bent of his later years, feeling that he was severing himself more and more from "that thick nourishing human air in which we all live and move." If she must be regarded as anyone's disciple, it would be more accurate to note her relation to George Eliot, whose clear, strong style, broad canvas, and obsession with moral questions always fascinated her.

As long as Mrs. Wharton had elected, after the war, to continue writing about the social life of a city that she had given up even visiting, she would have done better to restrict herself to the eras of its history with which she was acquainted. The four stories that make up *Old New York* (1924) evoke the atmosphere of the last century as successfully as anything in *The Age of Innocence*. But she was too concerned with the world around her to write only of the past. She wanted nothing less than to interpret the age in which she lived and to seek out the origin and cause of the increasing number of things in it that angered her. Also, her way of life had become expensive — a house north of Paris, another on the Riviera, twenty-two servants — and she needed a wider audience. To take advantage of the big pay of the American women's magazines, it was necessary to write about Americans of the moment.

The Glimpses of the Moon (1922) was first serialized in the *Pictorial Review*, which may give the clue to its author's remarkable lapse of style and taste. The jacket of the book depicts an Italian villa on Lake Como by moonlight to evoke the mawkish, gushing mood of an opening chapter which makes the reader rub his eyes and look again to be sure that he is dealing with Edith Wharton. Nick and Susy Lansing, two bright young penniless hangers-on of the international set, have married on the understanding that their bond may be dissolved at the option of the first to find a richer spouse. Nick is again the dilettante hero, writing a novel about Alexander the Great in Asia because it takes less research than an essay, but now, for the first time, reader and author see him from radically different points of view. To the reader he is, quite simply, an unmitigated cad, perfectly content to live in the borrowed houses of rich friends so long as his wife agrees not to steal the cigars or to take any overt part in the blindfolding of their hostesses' deceived husbands. On these two commandments hang all his law and his prophets, and when Susy has violated both (in each case, for his sake), he abruptly abandons her to pursue an heiress. It is impossible to imagine how Mrs. Wharton could have picked such a man as the hero of a romance unless she seriously believed that he represented what a gentleman had sunk to in the seventeen years which had elapsed since the publication of *The House of Mirth.* But could even Lawrence Selden have degenerated to a Nick Lansing? And could Lily Bart ever have stolen cigars? Surely the world had not been entirely taken over by the Lansings and their dismal set of international drifters who blur together in a maze of furs and jewels and yachts. Mrs. Wharton's preoccupation with vulgarity had for the moment vulgarized her perceptions.

The lapse in her style can be illustrated by contrasting three descriptions of ladies of fashion. The first is from *The House of Mirth.* Lawrence Selden is taking his shrewd, leisurely note of the person of Lily Bart, and his speculations provide our first insight into the central problem of her character: "Everything about her was at once vigorous and exquisite, at once strong and fine. He had a confused sense that she must have cost a great deal to make, that a great many dull and ugly people must, in some mysterious way, have been sacrificed to produce her. He was aware that the qualities distinguishing her from the herd of her sex were chiefly external: as though a fine glaze of beauty and fastidiousness had been applied to vulgar clay."

The second is from the scene in *Madame de Treymes,* published two years later, where John Durham contemplates Fanny de Malrive after her call upon his mother and sister at their hotel and discerns in her fluster a ground for hope as to his future. The passage, with a faint Jamesian ring, is finely conceived: "The mere fact of her having forgotten to draw on her gloves as they were descending in the hotel lift from his mother's drawing-room was, in this connection, charged with significance to Durham. She was the kind of woman who always presents herself to the mind's eye as completely equipped, as made of exquisitely cared for and finely-related details; and that the heat of her parting with his family should have left her unconscious that she was emerging gloveless into Paris, seemed, on the whole, to speak hopefully for Durham's future opinion of the city."

Turning to *The Glimpses of the Moon,* we see one of Susy Lansing's friends, not only through Susy's eyes, but through the angrily disapproving eyes of Mrs. Wharton. The idea to be conveyed is that the lady described is as banal as her motor and her motor as banal as a magazine advertisement, but as the style is literally the style of a magazine advertisement, we can only wonder what reason the author has to sneer: "But on the threshold a still more familiar figure met her: that of a lady in exaggerated pearls and sables, descending from an exaggerated motor, like the motors in magazine advertisements, the huge arks in which jeweled beauties and slender youths pause to gaze at snowpeaks from an Alpine summit."

Fortunately the novels that followed *The Glimpses of the Moon* are not all quite as slick. If they are not good novels, neither are they pot-boilers. But it seems a pity that Mrs. Wharton should have chosen to lay all the blame for the shapelessness of the postwar world on her native land. In book after book her complaints grow shriller and shriller until at last everything across the Atlantic is tainted with the same grotesque absurdity. She gives to her American towns such names as Delos, Aeschylus, Lohengrin, and Halleluja, and to their inhabitants, in their brief hours away from money-making, a total gullibility in dealing with religious and medical charlatans. Their fuzzy zeal for good causes envelops their hideous skyscrapers in a stifling cloud of euphoria. And the American face! How it haunts her! It is as "unexpressive as a football." It might have been made by "a manufacturer of sporting goods." Its sameness encompasses her "with its innocent uniformity." How many of such faces would it take "to make up a single individuality"? Years before, she had written to an English friend about James: "America can't be quite so summarily treated and so lightly dismissed as our great Henry thinks." Yet, reading her later novels, we can only wish that she had dismissed America altogether.

Kate Clephane in *The Mother's Recompense* (1925) returns to a society in New York which has ostracized her, as it ostracized Mrs. Lidcote in "Autre Temps," to find, unlike Mrs. Lidcote, that it *can* revise its judgments. She is completely accepted by the people who once cut her and thinks the less of them for their tolerance. She finds only one person in New York who seems to have any real moral fiber, and that is her daughter who, perhaps for the same reason, strikes the reader as a rather wooden girl. When Kate discovers that Anne is ignorantly about to marry her own former lover, she tries desperately to break up the match without telling the girl why and finally surrenders to the situation in order to avoid "sterile pain." But having renounced sterile pain for her daughter, she elects it for herself by refusing the offer of marriage from a devoted old admirer who has been shocked, but only momentarily, by her confession.

Mrs. Wharton resented the critics who deplored the ending of the book and spoke of the "densities of incomprehension" with which she now felt herself surrounded. The clue to Kate's sacrifice, she hinted, lies in the quotation from Shelley on the flyleaf: "Desolation is a delicate thing." My own interpretation is that Kate, imbued with the sensitivity of one who, like Mrs. Lidcote, has been broken on the wheel of a sterner age, feels more keenly than anyone else the horror of Anne's marriage. What she hates in the modern world is not so much that such things can happen as that people no longer really care that they do. Anne is caught in the situation of marrying her mother's lover because her mother has *had* a lover, and for that there must be expiation on the mother's part, alone in her shabby Riviera village, without the comfort of her old admirer. For Kate to go from the litter of fallen rose petals and grains of rice of her daughter's wedding to her own would be joining forces with the noisy, thoughtless world of vacuous toasts in which all delicacy of feeling has vanished. Those who believe in the old, harder standards must be willing to suffer alone, without sympathy or even comprehension. But this, evidently, is not sterile pain. Kate Clephane is intended to inhale a finer aroma from the bouquet of her loneliness than her daughter will ever know.

So far Mrs. Wharton had only skirmished with America. The story of the Lansings takes place in Europe, and Kate Clephane's drama is too much of the heart to have the locality of first importance. But she was preparing herself for a closer study of what had happened to America, and she had now spotted a type that she considered a representative victim of the disease of modern vulgarity, if, indeed, it was not the virus itself. Pauline Manford in *Twilight Sleep* (1927) is the daughter of an invader from Exploit who has first been married to a son of the age of innocence, Arthur Wyant. But time has profoundly altered both types. The invader's daughter is no longer prehensile or even crude; she has become bland and colorless and pointlessly efficient, building a life of public speeches and dinner parties around causes that she does not even try to understand, while Wyant, no longer the cool, well-dressed New York gentleman with a collector's eye for painting and porcelain, has degenerated to a foolish gossiping creature whom his wife has understandably divorced for a sneaky affair with his mother's old-maid companion. That is what has come of the merger of the old and new societies; it has cost each its true character. Pauline Manford, with invader's blood, has survived better than has Wyant, but hers is a lonely and precarious survival in a rosy cloud floating on an ether of fatuity from which she views with frightened eyes the moral collapse of her family. The invaders and their daughters have in common the faculty of immense preoccupation, the former with their businesses, the latter with their causes. But both are blinded to all that is beautiful or significant in the world around them by the dust stirred up by their febrile activities.

In Mrs. Manford Edith Wharton was groping at the outline of a well-known American phenomenon, the committeewoman who, married to a man who cares only for his business, seeks refuge in bogus utopias where beauty is expected to spring like a phoenix from the ashes of pain. If Mrs. Wharton had only stayed in America, how quickly she would have comprehended such a woman! But Mrs. Manford is nothing but a caricature, mixing up her speeches to the birth control league and the society for unlimited families, going to the "Busy Man's Christ" for "uplift" treatments and seeing her children only by secretarial appointment. Mrs. Wharton seems to have no sense of the violent resentment that may underlie such a woman's placid stare or of the hatred of spouse and possessive passion for offspring that her false air of good sportsmanship may conceal. The American committeewoman is not apt, like Mrs. Manford, to be surrounded by a family who regard her goings-on merely with a cheerful, amused tolerance. *Twilight Sleep* is a formidable battering ram used on a straw woman.

There was to be one more last grim sketch of the final decadence resulting from the now ancient merger between old New York and the invaders. In the short story "After Holbein," a senile Mrs. Jaspar sits down alone every night at the end of her great dining room table, imagining that she is still the hostess at a dinner party, while her smirking servants go through a pantomime of serving guests. Anson Warley, a veteran bachelor, dilettante, and diner out, who has scorned her parties in the days of her greatness, suffering now himself from loss of memory, goes to her house by mistake, and the two old broken-down creatures squeak and gibber together, drinking the soda water which they take for Perrier-Jouet and admiring flower vases stuffed with old newspapers. It has been said that there is no compassion in this story, but how much compassion does a short story need? It is a chilling, cleverly executed little piece, a sort of dance of death, pointing a grim moral in the ultimate inanity of two lives dedicated to the ceremonial of the dinner party.

American mothers she had now done, together with their husbands, both of the invader and dilettante variety, but what about children? They had never played much of a role in her books, as, indeed, they had played little in her life. Mrs. Winthrop Chanler, a long-time friend of Mrs. Wharton's, has written that she was actually afraid of them. But if she was ignorant of American nurseries and schools, she was very much aware of those pathetic little waifs, the products of multiple marriages, who were dragged about Europe in the wake of rich, pleasure-seeking parents and finally abandoned with governesses in seaside hotels. The various Wheater offspring in *The Children* (1928) have sworn to remain together under the lead of Judith, the eldest, in spite of what other custody arrangements their various parents and "steps" may make. The children are sometimes amusingly, sometimes touchingly drawn, but the sketches are still superficial and "cute," and the background of rich expatriate life in European resorts is filled in with the now heavy hand of her satire.

The more interesting though secondary topic of the book is the relationship between Rose Sellars, the quiet, gentle widow of exquisite tact, with whom I suspect Mrs. Wharton may have a bit identified herself, and Martin Boyne, again the tasteful middle-aged bachelor, who has made a fortune, like other Wharton heroes, offstage and has now plenty of time to idle abroad. Rose Sellars immediately understands and accepts the fact that Boyne's preoccupation with the Wheater children is, unknown to himself, a manifestation of his hopeless passion for little Judith. The novel was published in the year that followed Walter Berry's death, and the relationship between the two characters seems analogous to what may have existed between their creator and Berry: she, loving and eager, but restrained by the fear of embarrassing them both by a scene that might expose the small beer of his feeling, and he, detached but admiring, half disappointed and half irritated at his own inability to respond to a gratifying if sometimes cloying affection. It is tempting to speculate that Martin Boyne's fate is the author's revenge on his deceased counterpart. We leave him in the end, old and desolate, staring through a ballroom window at the beautiful Judith who, dancing with young men, is no longer even aware of his existence.

After *The Children* Edith Wharton embarked, although then in her late sixties, on the most ambitious experiment of her literary career: the fictional biography of a young middle-western American writer, Vance Weston, told in two novels: *Hudson River Bracketed* (1929) and *The Gods Arrive* (1932). She opens his story in a town which is, typically enough, called Euphoria and plunges fearlessly into details of middle-western life, as if Sinclair Lewis by dedicating *Babbitt* to her had given her some special insight into an area of America that she had never even seen. The result is as bad as might be expected, but Vance Weston soon leaves his hometown and comes to New York and an old house on the Hudson where his creator is on more familiar ground and where he meets a highly accomplished young lady, Halo Spear, who recites German poetry to him. "Just listen to the sound of the words," she says, when he protests his ignorance of the tongue.

It is easy to ridicule this long saga with its distorted picture of the New York publishing world, its uncouth young writers and artists ("Zola — who's he?" somebody yawned. "Oh, I dunno. The French Thackeray, I guess."), its irritatingly efficient heroine who can change travel accommodations and rent villas as easily as she can spout Goethe, its insensitive hero whose obsessive egotism becomes ultimately tedious, its ponderous satires of popular novelists and literary hostesses, but it nonetheless contains a strong picture of a young genius who educates himself and fights his way to literary success with a ruthlessness of which he is too preoccupied to be more than dimly aware. We sympathize when he is stifled in the ignorant, carping atmosphere of his invalid first wife's home and with his artist's need to rip away even at the most basic family ties. Here at last in Edith Wharton's fiction is a picture of a man. It may have all kinds of personal significance that he is neither a New Yorker nor a gentleman. As he develops cultivation in Europe, however, he develops some of the hardness of the older Wharton heroes, and when he leaves Halo at last for a round of parties in London, there is not much to choose between him and Martin Boyne. But that is in the second volume which, like so many sequels, should never have been written. Both reader and author have become bored with Vance. Yet one cannot but be impressed by the fund of creative energy that could produce such a book on such a subject in the author's seventieth year.

At the very end of her life Edith Wharton turned back once again to the rich field of her childhood memories, and immediately the shrill bitterness disappears, and the old, clear, forceful style is back to the aid of its mistress. If she had finished *The Buccaneers* (1938) it might well rank among the best of her work. The little band of social-climbing maidens who find New York too difficult and leave it to triumph in London are unique in her fiction as possessing both her approval and affection. Old New York seems merely petty and narrow now in the person of Mrs. Parmore, while the parvenu is actually given charm and vitality in that of Colonel St. George. The author's point of view is expressed by the English governess of the St. George girls, Laura Testvalley, an erudite but romantic spinster of Italian descent, a cousin of the Rossettis, who adores her covey of Daisy Millers and guides them up the slippery rungs of the London social ladder. Until the girls have achieved their titles the mood of the book is light and amusing; thereafter it becomes more serious. For they have, after all, missed happiness, and Nan, as the author's notebooks reveal, will find hers only by leaving the Duke of Tintagel for Guy Thwarte.

Mrs. Wharton had not only cast aside for once her disapproval of those who are discontented to remain in the social grade of their origin; she had even cast off four decades of classicism in taste and morals to plot an ending that was to celebrate the triumph of "deep and abiding love." Yet how many times in her stories and novels have we not been told that no love can survive the cold shoulder of society, the disintegrating shabbiness of a life in second-class watering places! And is Nan now to get away with it, to escape the fate of Anna Karenina?

But if Mrs. Wharton, at the end, permitted herself to indulge in the vision of a love that was to make up for everything, the love that Ellen Olenska and Newland Archer had renounced, she was still enough of a Yankee puritan to stipulate that such a love had to be paid for. If Nan and Guy are to have their happiness, Laura Testvalley must lose hers. Her engagement to Guy's father will not survive her role in his son's elopement. Laura, the author's representative and a bit her alter ego, must be sacrificed to the gods of order. One wonders if at the last those gods did not, to Laura's creator, show some of the lineaments of the gods of derision whom she had so bitterly apostrophized in her journal thirty years before.

With her posthumously published works, *The Buccaneers* and *Ghosts,* the total of Edith Wharton's fiction comes to thirty-two volumes. Obviously, her ultimate reputation in American letters will rest upon only a fraction of this list. *Ethan Frome,* I have no doubt, will always be read, but it is out of the main stream of her work. I believe that she will be remembered primarily for her two great novels of manners: *The House of Mirth* and *The Age of Innocence.* In these she succeeded in re-creating an unadventurous and ceremonious society, appropriately sheltered behind New York brownstone, looking always to the east rather than to the west, and the impact upon it of the winds that blew from both directions. There were plenty of minor writers who attempted to delineate this society, but among those of the first rank Mrs. Wharton, at least in the first decade of our century, had it to herself. It is true, of course, that some of James's characters come from the same milieu, but they are rarely considered in relation to their native land or cities. The reason Mrs. Wharton succeeded where so many others have failed is that in addition to her gifts as an artist she had a firm grasp of what "society," in the smaller sense of the word, was actually made up of. She understood that it was arbitrary, capricious, and inconsistent; she was aware that it did not hesitate to abolish its standards while most loudly proclaiming them. She knew when money could open doors and when it couldn't, when lineage would serve and when it would be merely sneered at. She knew that compromises could be counted on, but that they were rarely made while still considered compromises. She knew her men and women of property, recently or anciently acquired, how they decorated their houses and where they spent their summers. She realized that the social game was without rules, and this realization made her one of the few novelists before Proust who could describe it with any profundity. In American fiction her nearest counterpart is Ellen Glasgow.

Edith Wharton died in her house near Paris of a stroke in 1937, at the age of seventy-five. Her private papers were given to Yale and may not be published before 1968, which is probably the reason no biography has yet appeared. A great deal has been written about her in articles and memoirs, but almost always about the great lady, rarely the writer. This is nobody's fault, for Mrs. Wharton took a certain pride in keeping her writing behind the scenes, in presenting herself to the world, so to speak, on her own. One short piece, however, by Iris Origo, describes a weekend on Long Island that Mrs. Wharton spent with old friends during a brief visit to America to receive a degree from Yale. It is one of the rare recorded occasions when the survivor from New York's age of innocence, the real figure behind the novelist, predominated over the brilliant and formidable lady of perfect houses and gardens. Iris Origo relates how Mrs. Wharton refused to be led into any discussion of persons or events in France, of Carlo Placi or Madame de Noailles, and how, at each such attempt, she gently and firmly steered the conversation back to old friends and old memories in New York. The W's house on 11th Street, had it really been pulled down? Did her hostess remember the night they had dined there before the Colony Club ball? The X's daughter, the fair one, had she married her young Bostonian? Had Z indeed lost all his money?

"For the whole evening, this mood continued. At one moment only — as, the last guest gone, she turned half-way up the stairs to wave good-night — I caught a glimpse of the other Edith: elegant, formidable, as hard and dry as porcelain. Then, as she looked down on her old friends, her face softened, even the erectness of her spine relaxed a little. She was no longer the trim, hard European hostess, but a nice old American lady. Edith had come home."

3

ELLEN GLASGOW

ELLEN GLASGOW'S parents combined the qualities that gave to both antebellum and reconstructed Virginia its stubborn romanticism and its peculiar strength. Her father, of Valley stock, was an ironworks executive and a Scotch Presbyterian in every nerve and sinew; he gave his children all the things they needed but love, and in eighty-six years never "committed a pleasure." The best his daughter could say of him was that he had not hurt anyone for the mere satisfaction of hurting. Her mother, on the other hand, descended from Randolphs and Yateses, was a flower of the old Tidewater, who, smiling in the constant sadness of her tribulations, would have divided "her last crust with a suffering stranger." Miss Glasgow attributed the lingering, undiagnosed malady of which her mother ultimately died to the exhaustion of bearing ten children and the hardships of war and reconstruction, but it was more probably the result of the same nervous temperament that her daughter inherited. "Born without a skin," the young Ellen's Negro mammy, shaking her head, used to say of her charge.

But in 1873, the year of her birth, the worst, at least financially, was over. The Glasgows had, in addition to a town house in Richmond, the farm of Jerdone Castle where their daughter could range over wide fields, the greater part of which were left to run wild in

56

broomsedge and scrub pine and life-everlasting, and cultivate the love of natural things and the sense of kinship with birds and animals that were never to leave her. Too nervous to go regularly to any school, she educated herself by reading all the books in the family library, science and history as well as fiction and poetry. An older sister's husband, a scholar, made her study *The Origin of Species* till she knew "its every page." According to her posthumous and by no means modest memoirs, she seems as a young woman to have had her cake and swallowed it, for she "won all the admiration, and felt all the glorified sensations, of a Southern belle" while at the same time making acquaintance with the squalor of Richmond slums as a worker for the City Mission and becoming a "Fabian Socialist." One can assume, at least, that she was no ordinary debutante.

When her mother died in 1893 she was so prostrated with grief that she tore up the uncompleted manuscript of her first novel, *The Descendant,* and a year passed before she was able to turn back to writing. Something of the same paralyzing prostration was to follow, in later years, the deaths of her sister Cary and of the man described in her memoirs as "Gerald B_____." Miss Glasgow always regarded herself as a uniquely sensitive and unhappy person. Answering the question of how she had liked her life in 1934 she replied: "not one day, not one hour, not one moment — or perhaps, *only one* hour and one day." It was true that on top of the nervous headaches and attacks of her youth was loaded the burden of increasing deafness, but she was given the compensation of looks, wit, charm, gaiety (she was never one to wear her melancholy on her sleeve), friends innumerable, and a talent that was to grow in power through a long life almost to the end. She never married, but this was for no lack of opportunity. She broke two engagements and recorded that the maternal instinct, sacred or profane, had been left out of her nature.

Nor was she neglected by the reading public. Again and again she was a best seller. But the delay in the serious critical recognition to which she regarded herself as entitled rankled deeply. Believing that she was leading a literary crusade away from a sterile romantic tradition toward the presentation of the South in a realist manner, lightened by irony, she found it hard to be crossed off as a sentimental regionalist. That she obviously loved her native state and that her books sold by the thousands were perhaps enough to make her seem to the casual eye like the very thing that she abominated. And when she did break through the literary barriers with *Barren Ground* in 1925, she was already in her fifties and beginning to have a nostalgic eye for the old state of society against which she had rebelled. If she shuddered at Thomas Nelson Page, she shuddered more at *Sanctuary*. She might almost have said at the end, like that disillusioned Victorian, Rhoda Broughton: "I began life as Zola; I finish it as Miss Charlotte Yonge."

From the beginning she never wavered in her conviction that her role in life was to write novels — important novels. She kept a sharp eye on every development of her career, including all steps of publication, to ensure the unhampered growth of her reputation as a major novelist. She left Harper, which had published her first two novels, without a qualm (so far as appears in her correspondence) when she decided that Walter Hines Page at Doubleday would do a better job on the third, and after Doubleday had published sixteen of her titles (including a volume of poetry and another of short stories) she left it for Harcourt, Brace because she concluded that much of the Doubleday promotion which had helped to make her famous was "cheap." Similarly, although never rich, she did not hesitate, in the depths of the depression, to turn down an offer by *Good Housekeeping* of $30,000 to serialize *The Sheltered Life,* and she made a habit of seeking out critics to have the chance to present her literary case personally and to make perfectly clear what her books were about. In short, she was Ellen Glasgow's own best agent, as Amy Lowell had been Amy Lowell's.

Her first two novels, *The Descendant* (1897) and *Phases of an Inferior Planet* (1898), bristle with the young liberal's determination to be shockingly realistic and seem a bit jejune to modern eyes, but it should not be forgotten what a determined step away from romantic fiction, particularly on the part of a young woman gently bred, they must have represented to her contemporaries. If a southern lady produced novels at all, they were expected to deal with plantation life, either in its antebellum splendor or in heroic and picturesque decay.

Miss Glasgow's first two tales may seem as far from Faulkner as the sentimental tosh from which they were a reaction, and she herself in later years came to regard the so-called "honest" school of southern literature as a combination of everything that was "too vile and too degenerate to exist anywhere else," but there was nonetheless a strong historical link between the two.

It is a pity that she chose to lay the scene of both these novels in New York which she knew then only as an occasional visitor. Even later, when she had lived in the city for several years in succession, she never caught its flavor as she caught that of Williamsburg, Petersburg, and Richmond. She objected to being labeled a Virginia writer, and, indeed, her truths were universal, but it was still the case that they were better seen against a Virginia background. This, however, was to be no serious limitation, for hers was a diverse state, and she knew it thoroughly, its cities and its rural areas, its aristocrats and its businessmen, its politicians and its farmers. If she was a regionalist, she was a regionalist on a Trollopian scale.

The style of these early books combines the epigrammatic with the sentimental in a way that suggests a mixture of Meredith and Charlotte Brontë. Clever sentences like "Conscience represents a fetich to which good people sacrifice their own happiness, bad people their neighbors'" are to be found with such others as "It was the old, old expiation that Nature had demanded and woman paid since the day upon which woman and desire met and knew each other." Even more awkward is the intrusion into the supposedly free and easy life of the young bohemian characters of certain undiscarded standards of the author's Richmond upbringing. The radical hero of *The Descendant*, who preaches against marriage, is nonetheless still chaste when he meets and falls in love with an emancipated virgin to whom he protests: "I am not worthy to touch the hem of your garment." And Algarcife in *Phases of an Inferior Planet*, who loses his job in a women's college because of his articles on the "origin of sex," can still condemn his wife to bitter need rather than let her supplement the family income by taking a role in light opera. In bitter need, too, be it noted, they still have a "slipshod maid of work."

The important thing, however, to be observed about these forgotten little books is that, for all their crudenesses, they demonstrate a flow of narrative power and a vitality that show a young writer bound to make her mark. *The Descendant*, published anonymously, was by many attributed to Harold Frederic, which seems a greater compliment today than Miss Glasgow thought it at the time. In her middle twenties she was already established and could write Mr. Page about her third novel: "If the gods will it to be my last I don't want people to say 'she might have done big things,' because I am writing this book not to amuse, or to sell, but to *live,* and if it does so I shall be content not to — after it is finished."

The Voice of the People (1900), indeed, marks the real beginning of her career as a novelist. She had already conceived her master plan of writing "in the more freely interpretative form of fiction" a social history of Virginia from the decade before the Confederacy. Possibly using a bit of hindsight and showing that passion to see a lifework as centralized that characterizes the great French novelists, she later classified her fiction as fitting into the following categories and covering the following chronological periods:

History: *The Battle-Ground*, 1850–65; *The Deliverance*, 1878–90; *The Voice of the People*, 1870–98; *The Romance of a Plain Man*, 1875–1910; *Virginia*, 1884–1912; *Life and Gabriella*, 1894–1912.

Novels of the country: *The Miller of Old Church*, 1898–1902; *Barren Ground*, 1894–1924; *Vein of Iron*, 1901–33.

Novels of the city: *The Sheltered Life*, 1910–17; *The Romantic Comedians*, 1923; *They Stooped to Folly*, 1924; *In This Our Life*, 1938–39.

Actually, the only common denominator of all these novels is the Commonwealth of Virginia, as the only one that links the masterpieces of Zola's *Rougon-Macquart* is France in the Second Empire, but at least Miss Glasgow had the wisdom to rest her case on geography and did not try to connect her characters through the branches of an immense and exotic family tree.

The Voice of the People, although third in the history series, was the first to be published, because, unlike *The Battle-Ground* and *The Deliverance,* it required no research. Battle Hall might have been the

Jerdone Castle of Ellen Glasgow's own childhood, and we meet her for the first time as a writer in full possession of her native materials. She was to make Virginia the setting of all her subsequent novels but two: *The Wheel of Life* and *Life and Gabriella.* The first takes place totally in New York and is a total failure; the second takes place partly in New York and is in that part a failure. Without the Virginia that Miss Glasgow knew as a historian and felt as a poet, her characters never become fully alive.

As one first begins to succumb to the fascination of Battle Hall, with the visiting aunt who comes for a week and stays for years, with the miraculous reorganizing domestic powers of Miss Chris, with the friendly darkies and the long, succulent meals, with the rumbling memories in sleepy afternoons of more heroic days, one may start up and ask: How is all this so different from the romantic tradition? Isn't this more of Thomas Nelson Page? Perhaps. Miss Glasgow had a deeply ingrained sympathy for the antebellum aristocracy, but at the same time one begins to perceive the parts of the picture that her realist eye picks out: General Tom sinking into sloth and fantasy and the rigid standards of Mrs. Webb operating to depress and freeze people in their born stations. Nicholas Burr, the hero, of the poor white class, may educate himself, like Akershem in *The Descendant,* and may even rise to become governor of Virginia, and die a martyr's death holding off a lynching mob, but he fails to win Eugenia Battle, and his failure has been foreordained by the blind prejudice of her family.

Miss Glasgow's resolution of the class problem, however, is a bit muddied by her own preconceptions. One is willing to accept the fact that Nicholas Burr, like Akershem, is subject to violent fits of rage, and even to accept his rages as attributes of the uncivilized barbarian lurking in all of us, but one cannot as easily accept Miss Glasgow's complacent assumption that such violence lurks more insidiously in the lower orders. Why would not *any* man explode against a heroine who, without a hearing, blandly condemns him for the seduction of a farm girl who has in fact been seduced by the heroine's own brother? Yet Eugenia appears to have the author's sympathy when she finds in Nicholas' fury a "sinister" reminder of his father. And why sinister? Is his father an evil man? No, simply a vulgar one. Certainly there is here a tendency to equate violence with low birth and sex appeal, for the heroes of these early novels, however ugly of temper, have also some of the attributes of supermen. Later on, after a disillusioning personal experience, the men with whom Miss Glasgow's heroines become involved (no longer heroes by any stretch of the term) are weak, self-indulgent, and faithless. The confusion that exists in *The Voice of the People* was ultimately cleared up, but at the expense of the male sex.

Throughout this initial period of her literary career, Ellen Glasgow's hearing was steadily failing. As her income increased she began pilgrimages all over the world "more hopeless than the pilgrimages to shrines of saints in the Dark Ages," for there was no cure for the hardening in the Eustachian tube and the middle ear. Science had failed her body, she complained, as ruinously as religion had failed her soul, and she had to fall back on a humane stoicism and — ultimately — on golf. Deliberately she built "a wall of deceptive gaiety" around herself and cultivated the "ironic mood, the smiling pose." There was a surer refuge in mockery, she found, than in too grave a sincerity.

Romanticism, however, was still evident in *The Battle-Ground* (1902) which Alfred Kazin has called a "superior sword and cape romance based on the legend that the Civil War was fought between gentlemen and bounders." It is the only Glasgow novel where the action takes place before and during the Civil War and consequently before the author's own memory, which may explain why the early chapters are so filled with frothy chatter and gallantry, with toasts and boasts ("To Virginia, the home of brave men and of angels"), with loving loyal slaves and proud, high-tempered colonels. Of course, Miss Glasgow may have been deliberately intensifying the cavalier atmosphere in order to heighten the drama of the coming conflict that would sweep it all away. It has become the classic method of handling the opening of the Civil War, as seen in Margaret Mitchell's *Gone with the Wind* (a book which Miss Glasgow admired) and in Stephen Vincent Benét's *John Brown's Body*. It is, indeed, almost a literary convention to show the Confederacy dancing its way into disaster.

She did better, however, in the war chapters. Here she kept away as much as possible from battle scenes, for she never liked to write about things that she had not seen with her own eyes, and she concentrated on pictures, such as that of wartime Richmond, where her own hard research and contemporary knowledge could combine to give a proper focus. The novel ends where her real work in fiction begins: at the end of the war when the South faces the future in defeat. It is here that she establishes herself as totally distinct from those novelists who could only lament what had passed away and sigh over characters who did the same. Dan Montjoy, coming back to the ruins of his ancestral home, wounded and half-starved, can yet reflect that the memory of a beaten slave which used to haunt him need bother him now no more. And his grandfather, Major Lightfoot, who is unable mentally to take in the fact of Appomattox, augurs the postwar southern mental evasiveness about which Miss Glasgow was to have so much to say and to the exposure of which she was to devote her ironic art.

The Deliverance (1904) is her first fully mature work. It is a well-organized centripetal novel about impoverished aristocrats and unscrupulous parvenus in the era of reconstruction. For the first time Miss Glasgow was able to make effective use of the Virginia soil; and the tobacco fields which bring a fortune to Bill Fletcher, the embezzler who has robbed the Blake family of the plantation where he was once overseer, make a perfect setting for the bloody conflict between the still vigorous old order and the already decadent new, and for the terrible revenge of Christopher Blake who deliberately corrupts and destroys the ex-overseer's grandson. Miss Glasgow was to be outdone only by Willa Cather in her handling of rural atmosphere.

In her affection for the Blakes there is still a bit of nostalgia for antebellum days, but the bleak and closely observed present gives the twist of irony to all the memories and stories of that glorious era. The blind Mrs. Blake, whose family and servants together conspire to create in her sickroom the illusion of a victorious South, going so far as to invent names for the Confederate presidents of two postwar decades, is, of course, the symbol of the old South that rejected reality. Her son Christopher, on the other hand, who works in the tobacco fields to support the family, is an example of the aristocrat who has the courage to face and defeat poverty, even though born with the love of ease and the weakness to temptation in his blood, "with the love, too, of delicate food, of rare wines and of beautiful women." Did Miss Glasgow actually believe in the physical transmission of aristocratic characteristics? Evidently so, for Christopher, without education or other advantages, stands out among his fellow farmers as a natural leader. He is another of Miss Glasgow's supermen – he risks smallpox to bury the children of a former family slave – but he is even more irresistible to women than Nicholas Burr because of his noble birth, and when Maria Fletcher sees him, her creator's style slumps suddenly to the level of the lowest potboiler: "All the natural womanhood within her responded to the appeal of his superb manhood."

Maxwell Geismar has pointed out that Ellen Glasgow's novels are among our best sources of information on the southern mind because we can see in them the persistent imprint of primary cultural myths on even a perceptive and sophisticated talent. Miss Glasgow, he feels, for all her compassion and liberalism, could never quite free herself from her admiration of the old aristocracy with all its narrowness and prejudice. It is true. Negroes in her fiction are apt to appear as a carefree, feckless, lovable servant class whose peccadilloes and promiscuities are to be laughed at rather than condemned. In *One Man in His Time* she was actually able to write a whole book on the social problems facing a liberal governor of Virginia without mentioning the Negroes. She belonged, of course, to a generation that was taught to duck the problem in its cradle. But all this does not mean that she was unaware that it existed. Dan Montjoy in *The Battle-Ground* helps an escaped slave; Mrs. Pendleton in *Virginia* forces herself not to see the slave market; Dorinda Oakley in *Barren Ground* is a true friend of her Negro servant; Asa Timberlake in *In This Our Life* defies his family in order to protect a Negro boy from being framed for a crime. In this last episode Miss Glasgow does, if only for a few pages, face up to the fact that otherwise respectable white people may be willing to sacrifice an innocent colored boy to protect a vicious member of their own race. By and large, however, she did not choose to be overly concerned with the problem. She was one who felt that the modern Negro had lost the "spiritual" quality of his forebears, and she evaded the connection between such spirituality and bondage. She had her loves and her loyalties, and even at her most ironical there were certain boats that she was not going to rock.

In 1900 Ellen Glasgow met the man whom she describes as "Gerald B———" in her memoirs, and until his death seven years later she lived "in an arrested pause between dreaming and waking." As with "Harold S———," the other great love of her life, it was a case of opposites attracting. Gerald was a financier and a married man; they could meet only fleetingly and only on her visits to New York. One infers that the relationship was not happy, but it must have had its wonderful moments, and when he died of an inoperable ailment she was completely overwhelmed. If we are to take the relationship of Laura Wilde and Arnold Kemper in *The Wheel of Life*, a novel which she admittedly wrote as an antidote to her sorrow and later confessed to be in part autobiographical, as a picture of herself and Gerald, we thresh up an interesting speculation. Why was this woman, so dedicated to the mind and spirit, twice to fall in love with egocentric and hedonistic philistines? Was *this* what she meant by the indignities of the spirit to which she was so relentlessly subjected? It is difficult to imagine greater ones.

After receiving the news that Gerald was doomed, she records that she went up on a hillside in Switzerland and lay down on the grass where a high wind was blowing. There she had a mystical experience. "Lying there, in that golden August light, I knew, or felt, or beheld, a union deeper than knowledge, deeper than sense, deeper than vision. Light streamed through me, after anguish, and for one instant of awareness, if but for that one instant, I felt pure ecstasy. In a single blinding flash of illumination, I knew blessedness. I was a part of the spirit that moved in the light and the wind and the grass. I was — or felt I was — in communion with reality, with ultimate being. . . ." Something very like this experience was to go into the making of *Barren Ground* and *The Sheltered Life*.

In the terrible years that followed Gerald's death she became engaged to a man with whom she was never in love, but who offered her everything that her love for Gerald missed: "intellectual congeniality, poetic sympathy, and companionship which was natural and easy, without the slightest sting of suspicion or selfishness." Everything, in short, but delight and joy. His letters, those of a poet, stirred in her no greater emotion than gratitude. She asked herself if she had failed because she had preferred the second best in emotion, just as her fellow countrymen so often preferred the second best in literature. Perhaps she had, but the fact that she could see the irony of her situation was the rock on which she would later build her Queenborough trilogy.

In *The Wheel of Life* (1906), conceived in a mystical mood, poet Laura Wilde and her mentor Roger Adams struggle toward the recognition that man's only valid purpose is to identify himself with God and to lose his ego. The pursuit of happiness, even in love — love, in Laura's case, for a man, Arnold Kemper, who, however inconstant, sincerely offers marriage — is simply an invitation to disillusionment and betrayal. This is a theme that will constantly be met again in Ellen Glasgow's work. The most that a woman can expect from love is the opportunity to develop her character by facing inevitable abandonment with fortitude. It is a dreary credo, and enveloped in the somber atmosphere of *The Wheel of Life*, it makes for dreary reading. Laura's collapse into a living death when she discovers that she no longer loves Kemper is so humorlessly described that it engenders no sympathy. And worst of all, this quiet little drama of the soul is played out in New York, with none of the powerfully evoked landscapes of the Virginia novels. Miss Glasgow could never seem to get interested in describing Manhattan. It is always a cold, shadowy island seen only in terms of directions, "east along Sixty-sixth Street," "west to Fifth Avenue." Nor are even the minor characters indigenous. Angela Wilde, who never leaves her house, hovering upstairs like a wraith because she was compromised in her youth, is more Richmond than New York (we will meet her in later Glasgow fiction), and her senile brother who likes to play the flute seems a faded descendant from the gentle family of Dickensian lunatics.

A Virginia setting makes *The Ancient Law* (1908) better reading, but it is again the inferior product of a depressed period. Novels about saints are apt to be tedious, and Daniel Ordway, born in the arid tradition of those austere heroes of George Eliot, Felix Holt and Daniel Deronda, is not made more credible by having been, like another library model, a convict. The end of the book seems almost designed as a parody of nineteenth-century fictional saints. Ordway, having taken upon his own shoulders the guilt of his daughter's forgery, leaves his home a second time in disgrace and travels back to Tappahannock, the town which under an alias he has redeemed and made prosperous (compare *Les Misérables*), just in time to purchase the steel mills from the villain and save them from destruction by a mob of furious strikers to whom he promises fair hours and wages and by whom he is hailed in a final apotheosis. There was a curious streak of the preacher in Ellen Glasgow, quite at odds with her natural skepticism and ironical humor, that tended to seize upon her in her low moments.

The Romance of a Plain Man (1909) finds her happily back on the main avenue of a career which, almost uniquely among those of American writers, was to improve in quality (except for two long hiatuses caused by mental depression) until her old age. For the first and the last time in a novel she adopted the stratagem of the hero narrator, which disembarrassed the author of all problems as to points of view. She violated, however, the literary principle attached to its use: that everything to be told can be naturally told by the narrator. One does not believe, for example, that Ben Starr, who is announced in the title itself as a "plain man" and who has had to make his way up a rough business ladder from lower-middle-class rags to upper-middle-class riches, would describe breezes as being "fragrant with jessamine" or air as "heavy with the perfume of fading roses." Nor does one believe that Miss Glasgow ever intended him to sound as fatuous as he does when he notes that "I, the man of action, the embodiment of worldly success, was awed by the very intensity of my love."

Yet Ben's conquest of Sally Mickleborough's world is well described, and the best thing about it is that he can never make himself realize that he *has* conquered it. He feels that he must go on making money for Sally even when he suspects — or ought to suspect — that she wants only his love. But that, of course, is just Miss Glasgow's point: that he isn't really making money for her, but only to prove to himself that he is as good as her aunts and even as good as the great General Bolingbroke. He has been made to feel too deeply his own social inferiority as a child to imagine that it could ever be hidden by anything but a wall of gold. It is thus that materialism engenders materialism; in the end, when there is almost no hope left for the Starrs' happiness, Ben at last sees that the real division between himself and Sally has come "not from the accident of our different beginnings but from the choice that had committed us to opposite ends." It is Ben who ultimately insists on the importance of class as rigidly as Sally's Aunt Mitty Bland who has contemptuously remarked, when urged to concede the physical strength and stature of her proposed nephew-in-law: "What are six feet, two inches without a grandfather?"

Miss Glasgow was very sensitive to social changes; she saw and took it on herself to record that all over the South, as the industrial system displaced the agrarian aristocracy, men like Ben Starr were forging their way into prominence. She was perfectly willing to welcome them and to give them their due, perhaps even more, for she endows Ben with a touch of her old supermen when he knocks down a man whom he finds beating a horse. But she was handicapped in the business scenes by her ignorance of financial matters. Ben's money dealings are misty, which is again the fault of the narrator technique. He cannot talk about things that his creator did not understand, yet one knows that such a man would never stop talking about his big deals. Perhaps if one saw him through the eyes of Sally, who hated business, this part of the book would be more convincing. Edith Wharton, by showing her tycoons only at parties in *The House of Mirth*, was able to conceal from her reader an ignorance of stock exchange matters as deep as, if not deeper than, Miss Glasgow's. The latter should have done some of the research that Theodore

Dreiser did for his Cowperwood novels before letting Ben Starr tell
his own story.

If Ben Starr has risen, however, the old order has by no means
collapsed. Ben's greatest ambition is to rise only as high as General
Bolingbroke, a Civil War hero and aristocrat who has turned in his
later years to business to lead the South out of defeat. The General,
one of Miss Glasgow's most vivid characters (he cannot allow Miss
Matoaca Bland to criticize a politician's immoral life because he cannot allow that she should know that it existed), achieves independence from his own caste by sheer success. Having been exalted in
war as well as in peace, having been a leader in the old plantation
days as well as the smoky industrial new ones, he, alone of the characters, can see how fluctuating and passable are class lines. He can
see what Sally's aunts can never see, that Ben Starr will ultimately
change his class with his clothes and that only a few old maids will
oppose him to the end.

The Miller of Old Church (1911) marks Ellen Glasgow's coming of age, her advent as a major talent in American fiction. It
dramatizes the same rise of the lower middle class as *The Romance
of a Plain Man*, but it does so more effectively because the scene
is laid in a rural area. Miss Glasgow knew a lot more about millers
than she knew about financiers. The drama, too, is intensified by
the fact that the upper class here is declining. Ben Starr and General
Bolingbroke go forward, so to speak, hand in hand, but the Revercombs on the way up meet and clash with the declining Gays. This
makes for a better story, though on a more fundamental level it is
the soil, as opposed to the cobblestones of Richmond, that gives the
deeper interest. The Revercombs triumph over the Gays because
they have stronger roots. We have already seen that rural aristocrats
can hold their position only, like Christopher Blake in *The Deliverance*, by turning to the land. In making her point Miss Glasgow
occasionally allows us a glimpse of George Eliot and Thomas Hardy
looking over her shoulder, and Jonathan Gay's seduction of Blossom
Revercomb is a little too reminiscent of both *Adam Bede* and *Tess
of the d'Urbervilles*. She was to assimilate more entirely the bleak

morality of her great predecessors when she brought her own to its most effective expression in *Barren Ground*.

The Miller of Old Church shows some of the bluntness of style of Miss Glasgow's earlier days, and the omniscient author continues from time to time to obtrude a bit clumsily on the scene. One feels oneself back in the author's workshop on learning, of Abel Revercomb, that "essentially an idealist, his character was the result of a veneering of insufficient culture on a groundwork of raw impulse," or of Molly that "a passing impulse was crystallized by the coldness of her manner into a permanent desire." But in the delineation of Mrs. Gay, Ellen Glasgow was writing as well as she would ever write. It is the revenge of her aristocrats that even slipping they dominate the scene. Mrs. Gay is everything that old Virginia wanted a woman to be — lovely, helpless, indolent, and ignorant, and she conceals behind these qualities an inner force that enchains and destroys all those around her: her brother-in-law, his mistress, her sister Kesiah (a magnificent portrait of an ugly old maid rejected by a world that idolizes beauty), and finally her own son. The last chapter, where after the catastrophe of Jonathan's murder the characters raise their arms in a paean of praise to the wonder of his mother's fortitude, the same mother whose selfishness and prejudice have caused the tragedy, is the first great triumph in Miss Glasgow's use of irony.

The Mrs. Gays of Virginia, however, were not always destructive. Sometimes they were heroic, in which case, poor creatures, they found themselves, by the turn of the century, harmless anachronisms. Such a one is the heroine of *Virginia* (1913), the first of Ellen Glasgow's great tragicomedies. The amazing thing about the character of Virginia Pendleton is that, loyal, sweet, brave, unimaginative, and uncomplaining, she bores everybody but the reader. In this she surpasses Thackeray's Amelia who bores everybody but Dobbin. She is brought up to be the model wife that every southern gentleman was supposed to desire, and may have desired — twenty years before her birth. She admires her husband without comprehending him or without even trying to. She is gentle when a lady should be gentle but capable of a pioneer woman's strength in adversity. Like her old schoolmistress, the embattled spinster Priscilla Batte, she is capable "of dying for an idea but not of conceiving one." She is ignorant, pure, and beautiful, a rose of the Tidewater, but fascinating to meet — in a novel.

From the very beginning of this admirable book, Virginia's parents and teachers are perfectly united in their unconscious aim of turning her into a creature bound to be blighted by the world in which she must live. Her only hope would have been to find a husband (and there were such) who had been in his turn educated to appreciate her type. But, ironically enough, it is old Priscilla Batte herself who, incapable of envisaging any nice young man who would not cherish Virginia, deliberately stimulates the interest of Oliver Treadwell in this finest flower of her educational garden. From the moment she does so the novel moves as relentlessly to its conclusion as if it had been conceived by Flaubert or Zola. Virginia's undiscriminating adoration ends by driving her husband to New York and another woman, and when he has gone she has nothing to fall back on but the same commodious attic of fortitude that sustained her mother through the dreary years of war and reconstruction. But military defeat is easier to bear than desertion, and Virginia's cup is bitterer than her parents'.

She does, however, have one consolation, her son Harry, who in the last paragraph of the book telegraphs that he is coming back from Europe to be with her. One does not feel that it is quite fair of Miss Glasgow to leave us on this enigmatic note. Might Virginia not become a worse fiend than Mrs. Gay and ruin Harry's life by a possessiveness disguised as unselfishness? Would that not be just the revenge that her type might unconsciously take on a world and a sex that had let her down?

Virginia is addressed to a social problem that had largely been solved at the time of its publication, for Miss Priscilla Batte and her academy for preserving the natural ignorance of young ladies belonged to an earlier generation. Yet it is hard to imagine a more effective illustration of the romanticism and intransigency of the South which had certainly not disappeared in 1913. When asked what the South needed Miss Glasgow once quipped: "blood and irony." The latter she was to supply in increasing doses, but first was to come the second of those hiatuses in her literary development.

The death of her sister Cary in 1911 was followed by a period of depression in which much of *Virginia* was written. Fortunately for that book it had been conceived and commenced before the final blow, and the writing of it acted as a kind of therapy for her grief. But *Life and Gabriella* (1916), having its birth in a time of desolation, is the arid product of a preoccupied imagination. It is as if Ellen Glasgow were saying over and over again with an almost psychotic monotony: "It does not matter what happens to one, so long as one has fortitude, so long as one is not crushed by life." If Mrs. Gay is the weak and selfish Virginia woman and if Virginia Pendleton is the good and crushed one, Gabriella is the Virginia woman triumphant over all obstacles. The obstacles, indeed, bend like rushes before the storm of her resolution.

Her story reads like the outline of a novel with all the author's notes unerased. The very subtitle, *The Story of a Woman's Courage*, suggests a juvenile. Gabriella Carr, after a few vivid chapters describing the desperate life of decayed gentlewomen in Richmond, is captured by the charms of a New Yorker, George Fowler, marries him, and goes to live in his native city. His charms must be accepted because Miss Glasgow insists upon them. They are not otherwise apparent, though his magnetism is faintly suggestive of Arnold Kemper's in *The Wheel of Life* and may have the same source. When we first see Gabriella and George together we are told in the heaviest of asides that "In his eyes, which said enchanting things, she could not read the trivial and commonplace quality of his soul." George, in the now habitual way of Glasgow men, deserts her, and Gabriella, with serene faith in her own capacities, takes over the management of a flourishing dress shop and, after a brief struggle with her old Dominion blood, marries Ben O'Hara, another lowly born superman who has passed the hero's test by rescuing an asphyxiated woman and her small children from a burning house.

Another unfortunate thing about this novel is that the author's snobbishness is among the notes that she failed to erase. Gabriella's difficulties in bringing herself to accept the Irishman are understandable in a woman of her background, but her attitude toward the newly rich whom she meets at Mrs. Fowler's dinners is based on a pride of birth that the author seems to find quite acceptable. To Miss Glasgow as well as to her heroine it is inconceivable that Mrs. Fowler, "with the bluest blood of Virginia in her veins, should regard with such artless reverence the social activities of the granddaughter of a tavern-keeper." If Mrs. Fowler is going to be a snob, in other words, she should go about it in a larger spirit!

American involvement in World War I and Miss Glasgow's infatuation with the "Harold S——" of the memoirs came at the same time, and neither event helped to get her out of the slump of this period. It was obviously humiliating for the possessor of an eye so keen to irony to have to turn it on herself and her lover, but turn it she did in the pages of her memoirs. There is nothing sharper or more devastating in all her fiction than the picture of Harold in *The Woman Within*. Everything that she despised most in life — trivial honors, notoriety, social prominence, wealth, fashion, ladies with titles, the empty show of the world — he adored, and she loved him in spite of it for nothing more than a "defiant gaiety" that piqued her interest. Only when, on a Red Cross mission to the Balkans, he had acted out against a background of war horrors his grotesque parody of a Graustarkian romance with Queen Marie of Romania was she partially cured of her infatuation. But in the despair that followed this episode she took an overdose of sleeping pills, not caring if she lived or died.

She lived, and there was left the war. Even worse for her fiction than her passion for the "pluperfect snob" was her vicarious suffering over distant carnage. This produced her worst novel, if a political tract full of Wilsonian idealism can be called a novel at all. *The Builders* (1919) grew out of the same shrill war feeling that produced Edith Wharton's *A Son at the Front*. David Blackburn, a waxwork Rochester, harangues his child's nurse, Caroline Meade, a rather testy Jane Eyre, on the sad state of the solid South, the evils of the one-party system, and the need for a league of nations. "The future of our democracy," he writes her in his first love letter, "rests not in the halls of Congress but in the cradle, and to build for per-

manency we must build, not on theory, but on personal rectitude."
Angelica Blackburn's wickedness and her success in playing the in-
jured wife provide what little story there is, but even this is spoiled
by the clumsy device of having the reader see her first through Caroline's eyes as a noble, suffering creature. It is so manifest that she
is not this that we brand Caroline as a ninny, and the central point
of view of the novel is hopelessly discredited.

The almost immediate disillusionment that came to so many after
the Armistice came to Ellen Glasgow, and one suspects that she was
soon a bit ashamed of *The Builders*. Certainly there is no trace of
David Blackburn's exalted idealism in *One Man in His Time* (1922).
It is not a good novel, but it is at least a novel, and there must have
been those who wondered, after its predecessor, if she would ever
write one again. Gideon Vetch, the poor white who has risen to be
governor of Virginia, is a man who believes that the end justifies the
means, but at least he believes in an end, and he dies, assassinated,
the victim of the rising underdogs and the static "haves," the second
Glasgow hero to suffer a violent end in this high but evidently dangerous office. For the first time in her fiction Miss Glasgow paid
serious attention to her points of view and handled them with some
degree of subtlety. Vetch is never seen directly, but always through
the eyes of others, hostile or admiring, which lends a needed suspense to his story.

Other than Vetch, however, this book, like *Gabriella* and *The
Builders*, is thin. One feels that Miss Glasgow shares Corinna Page's
feeling about the hero: "She had a sincere though not very deep
affection for Stephen." Stephen Culpeper is too much under the influence of his vapid mother to have been the war hero he is reputed.
One does not believe that it took such valiance in 1920 for a young
man to marry the daughter of the governor of Virginia simply because Patty Vetch's mother had reportedly been a circus rider. And
his awakening to human misery after a single tour of the slums of
Richmond is a turgid interruption of the story, as is the melodramatic
episode when Patty, who does not know she is adopted and thinks
her mother dead, visits her "aunt," actually her mother, now a dope
fiend. But at least one feels in the pulse of the novel that Ellen Glas-

gow was emerging from the second period of despond in which she had been so long engulfed.

The best thing about her life was that the best part of it came after the age of fifty. As she wrote herself: "After those intolerable years, all my best work was to come." Her parents were dead, as were Cary and Gerald, and she was largely cured of Harold. She was alone now in the old gray Georgian house with the great tulip poplars at One West Main Street, except for her companion, Anne Virginia Bennett, who had come as a trained nurse and stayed to be a secretary. She regretted the absence of literary life in Richmond, but it was the world in which she had grown up and from which she drew much of her inspiration. It was home, and a home, too, where she was increasingly admired and respected. When she went out to parties, she talked, as she described it, of "Tom, Dick, and Harry," but why not? The real life was within. And what did Tom, Dick, and Harry matter when she was entering the finest part of her career?

Barren Ground (1925) shows the influence of Hardy at last assimilated. Egdon Heath is not more part of the lives of the characters of *The Return of the Native* than is the Piedmont countryside part of the lives of the Oakleys. Its flatness creates the illusion of immensity, and the broomsedge spreads in smothered fire over the melancholy brown landscape to a bleak horizon. The colors are fall colors from autumnal flowers: the crimson sumach, the wine-colored sassafras, the silvery life-everlasting. The Oakleys themselves are "products of the soil as surely as were the scant crops." Joshua looks heavy and earthbound even in his Sunday clothes; for all his scrubbing the smell of manure clings to him; and when Dorinda walks in the October countryside she feels her surroundings so sensitively that "the wall dividing her individual consciousness from the consciousness of nature vanished with the thin drift of woodsmoke over the fields." The inanimate character of the horizon becomes as personal, reserved, and inscrutable as her own mind.

Even the morality springs from the soil, or rather from man's battle with it. The broomsedge is the eternal enemy, always ready to engulf every new farm and field, and men are graded by how they fight it. "For it was not sin that was punished in this world or the

next; it was failure. Good failure or bad failure, it made no difference, for nature abhorred both." Jason Greylock, Dorinda's lover in
her youth, is weak, and he is broken and finally in dying becomes a
lesser thing than the soil; he is identified with a thistle. Dorinda in
her fortitude, a Glasgow fortitude built on Jason's desertion, tri-
umphs over the land and builds a dairy farm where the broomsedge
was. After the death of her husband, Nathan Pedlar, married for
convenience, and of Jason, Dorinda embraces the land anew. Perhaps Miss Glasgow is a bit carried away by her theme here: "The
storm and the hag-ridden dreams of the night were over, and the land
which she had forgotten was waiting to take her back to its heart.
Endurance. Fortitude. The spirit of the land was flowing into her,
and her own spirit, strengthened and refreshed, was flowing out again
toward life."

Aside, however, from a few such overladen passages and the old
habit of dwelling at too great length on her heroine's suffering in
abandonment, *Barren Ground* is her finest work. She achieves a
greater unity than in the earlier books by strictly limiting the points
of view. The central struggle in the story is between Dorinda and the
soil, and we see it entirely through Dorinda's mind except when the
author intervenes to supplement our picture of the countryside and
Pedlar's Mill. In this the technique is not unlike Flaubert's in *Madame Bovary* where, as Percy Lubbock has pointed out, we have to
see only two things: Yonville as it looks to Emma Bovary and Yonville as it looks to Flaubert. Actually, there is much less of the author
in *Barren Ground* because Dorinda, unlike Emma, is a woman of
enough perception to give us most of the necessary impressions herself.

Miss Glasgow maintained that the Abernethys (Dorinda's mother
was an Abernethy), the Greylocks, and the Pedlars were representative of a special rural class, not "poor whites" but "good people"
and descendants of English yeomen, who had never before been
treated in fiction. She gains greatly in the vividness of her portrayal
by not mixing them with characters of other backgrounds. Everyone
we see in Pedlar's Mill belongs in Pedlar's Mill like the broomsedge,
and the only chapters that mar the otherwise perfect unity of mood

in this beautifully conceived novel are those where Dorinda goes to New York to work for a doctor. The Manhattan setting is, as usual, fatal to Miss Glasgow's fiction.

She now embarked on her great trilogy of Richmond, or "Queenborough": *The Romantic Comedians* (1926), *They Stooped to Folly* (1929), and *The Sheltered Life* (1932). The three books do not constitute a trilogy in the sense that they have a continuous plot or even characters in common, but they share a common setting and class, the latter being the old but still prosperous Richmond families, and a spirit of ironic high comedy. They also share — and this is a fault if they are read consecutively — a hero, at least to the extent that the elderly man who is the principal observer in each has a melancholy sense of having missed the real fun in life. It is confusing that they are so alike yet not the same. Miss Glasgow never hesitated to plagiarize herself.

Turning from *Barren Ground* to *The Romantic Comedians* is like turning from Hardy to Meredith, from *The Return of the Native* to *The Egoist*. It is one of the great tours de force of American literature. "After I had finished *Barren Ground*," she wrote in her preface, "which for three years had steeped my mind in the sense of tragic life, the comic spirit, always restless when it is confined, began struggling against the bars of its cage." Never was it to escape to greater advantage. Judge Honeywell, surrounded and tormented by women, is surely one of the most amusing studies in southern fiction. His outrageous twin sister, Edmonia Bredalbane, who wears her scarlet letter as if it were a decoration, his old sweetheart, Amanda Lightfoot, the eternally brave and sweet "good" woman, whose life is a ruin because she could never face a fact, and his dead wife whose image wears a halo of oppressive rectitude, would all keep him from the folly of turning to a girl forty years his junior, but the benighted old fool has had enough of them (who wouldn't?) and wants one joy, one real joy of his own, before the end. The reader knows, everyone knows, even the judge, deep down, knows that this joy will turn to brambles, but he *will* have his way and does. The young wife, Annabel, is just right, too, for she has all the selfishness of youth and all its charm, and we expect her to find her marriage impossible. There is a tragic tone to the book, but it is never allowed to become heavy. The laughter, even when muted almost to a compassionate silence, is still there.

Ellen Glasgow was now in her early fifties and beginning prematurely to suffer from the tendency of so many older people to find youth without standards and to deplore the loss of disciplines in the world about her. It was the same tendency that spoiled so much of the later fiction of Edith Wharton. Miss Glasgow's correspondence is now increasingly full of complaints about the sloppiness and sordidness of modern living and modern literature. She came to look back on her own past, which she had found so stultifying as a girl, with increased nostalgia as she saw the effects of the new liberty of deportment and the new realism of expression that she had herself espoused. Once the note of shrillness, even of petulance, had entered her fiction it could only be lost when, as in *The Sheltered Life* and in the early chapters of *Vein of Iron*, she moved her setting back prior to those ills with which she now saw the world inundated.

They Stooped to Folly is the first of her books to suffer from this lack of sympathy with young people. The youthful characters are hard, angular, and unconvincing. Millie Burden, with the monotony of a minor character in Dickens, repeats over and over that she is "entitled to her life." Mary Victoria is so repellently fatuous and egocentric that she has to be kept off the scene if we are to believe, as the author insists that we shall, in her great influence over other people. And Martin Welding is too weak and self-pitying to cause the havoc he is supposed to cause in female hearts.

The novel as a whole seems like a compilation of discarded sketches from the atelier that produced its happier predecessor. Virginius Littlepage is a small, stuffy version of Judge Honeywell, and nothing happens to him except that he loses his unloved but superior spouse during and not before his chronicle. There is no Annabel for him, only a flirtation with a gay widow that makes him ridiculous but never pathetic. It is impossible to believe in his great love for his daughter Mary Victoria, whose meanness he sees as clearly as does the reader, or in his great sorrow over her obviously doomed marriage to a man whom she has ruthlessly torn from another woman. It is difficult, in fact, for the reader not to feel that all of the Littlepages deserve anything they get.

So what is left? Nothing but epigrams, and even these are repetitive. The characters cannot seem to make their points too often. Millie Burden talks only of her "rights," and her mother only of Millie's need for punishment. Mrs. Littlepage keeps insisting that she has never known her husband to be sarcastic, whereas the reader has never known him to be anything else. And what is the theme of it all? That a woman should not be punished all her life for having lived with a man out of wedlock! What can Miss Glasgow have thought she was up to? Nobody *is* so punished in the book, except Aunt Agatha, and that was in the ancient past. And nobody in the book thinks anyone *should* be so punished except Mrs. Burden, and she is represented as an absurd anachronism. Why then, in 1929, did the author keep flogging so dead a horse? Is it possible that she was beginning to feel that the age of prejudices had at least had standards? That one could only have ladies if one burned witches?

They Stooped to Folly cleared out the author's atelier of all these rag ends, for the last volume of the trilogy, *The Sheltered Life*, is a masterpiece. "In *Barren Ground*, as in *The Sheltered Life*," she wrote, "I have worked, I felt, with an added dimension, with a universal rhythm deeper than any material surface. Beneath the lights and shadows there is the brooding spirit of place, but, deeper still, beneath the spirit of place there is the whole movement of life." It is not a modest statement, but Miss Glasgow felt that she had worked too hard to have time for modesty, and certainly these two novels have a vibration different from all her others.

Into the double, battered stronghold of the Archbalds and Birdsongs on Washington Street, now all commercial but for them, creeps the fetid smell of the neighboring chemical plant. The smell is more than the modern world that threatens them from without; it is the smell of the decadence that attacks them from within. The sheltered life is also the life of willful blindness; the two families resist change and resist facts. Eva Birdsong, keeping up the queenly front of a Richmond beauty, tries not to see that her husband is a hopeless philanderer. General Archbald, dreaming of a past which he understands, avoids the duty of facing a present which he does not, while his daughter-in-law brings up little Jenny Blair to be a debutante of the antebellum era. Etta, the hypochondriac, lives in a fantasy world of cheap novels and heroes, and Birdsong, in the arms of his Negro mistress, imagines that he still loves his wife. The rumbles of a world war are heard from very far off. Like the smell down the street they do not yet seem to threaten the sheltered lives of the Archbalds and Birdsongs.

The terrible story that follows is seen from two points of view, General Archbald's and Jenny Blair's, those of age and youth. The General's long reverie into his own youth, "The Deep Past," is probably the finest piece of prose that Miss Glasgow ever wrote. The picture of a nauseated child being "blooded" by his sporty old grandfather on a fox hunt is for once without sentiment for the great Virginia days. Like Judge Honeywell and Virginius Littlepage, General Archbald has missed the high moments of life and has been married, like all elderly Glasgow gentlemen, to a good woman whom he did not love. He has been a gentleman and done his civic duty because, in the last analysis, nothing else seemed any better or certainly any finer, but he has a much deeper sense of what is wrong with his world than the other two heroes of the trilogy and a mystic sense that in death he may yet find the ecstasy that he has lost without ever possessing. Under the prosperous attorney and the member in good standing of the Episcopal church is a poet. If he were not quite so old, he might have saved his granddaughter.

But nobody is going to do that. Jenny Blair, brought up in innocence by her gallant widowed mother, cannot believe herself capable of doing anything that is not quite nice. She is drawn into an entanglement with Mr. Birdsong because she will not see that adultery is something that could happen to her. She is a little girl, even at eighteen, a bright, innocent, enchanting little girl, and the subtlest thing in this subtle book is that even while we keep seeing the small events of Washington Street from her point of view, we gradually become aware that others are beginning to see her differently, that John Welch, the Birdsongs' ward, suspects what she's up to, that Birdsong is aware that she's tempting him, that even her mother and grandfather begin to sense a change. The warnings proliferate, and the tempo of the book suddenly accelerates until the vision of Jenny Blair as a sharp-toothed little animal, free of all rules and restraints, reaching out to snatch the husband of her desperately ill friend, bursts upon us in its full horror, just before the final tragedy. Eva Birdsong shoots her husband, and his body slumps in the hall amid the carcasses of the ducks that he has killed. It is the ultimate drama-tization of the divorce between the Virginian myth and the Virginian fact, the climax of the novel and of Ellen Glasgow's fiction.

John Welch is the best of youth, as Miss Glasgow was coming to see youth, but he is a dry young man, tough and belligerently unsentimental. In assessing Eva Birdsong's chances of surviving her operation he mentions to General Archbald that her kidneys are sound. It is not, of course, agreeable to this gentleman of the old school to hear a lady's vital organs spoken of as plainly as if they were blocks of wood, but he reflects that perhaps such blunt-ness is the better way, that "wherever there is softness, life is cer-tain to leave its scar." In this he is certainly the spokesman for his creator who felt that all her life she had been constantly soft and constantly wounded, but there is no question of where her sympa-thies lay. For all her expressed tolerance of Welch and his contem-poraries, they lay with the General, and with her sympathies went the conviction that the suffering life was the richer one.

Two more novels were to follow *The Sheltered Life*, but they show an attenuation of powers. *Vein of Iron* (1935) seems a hol-low echo of *Barren Ground*. It starts well enough, for it starts in the past where as an older woman Miss Glasgow was increasingly at home, and deals with people whom she had not treated before, the descendants of the Scotch-Irish settlers in the southern part of the Virginia Valley. This was where her father's people had come from, and she was able effectively to evoke in the early chapters the bare, grim Presbyterian elements of the Fincastle family and their village, called, with a labored appropriateness, Ironside. The characters who are hard are very hard, and those who are stoical are very stoical, and even the names of the surrounding geographical features sug-gest the somber spiritual atmosphere in which these joyless people live: God's Mountain, Thunder Mountain, Shut-in Valley. Mobs of shrieking children cast pebbles at idiots and unmarried mothers alike, though there are few of the latter, as a girl need only point to the man actually, or allegedly, responsible to have him dragged to the altar by her fellow villagers. It seems possible that Miss Glasgow may have written a bit too much of her father's character into Ironside, but the result is very much alive. Such cannot be said of the second part of the novel where the characters move to Queenborough and to the present. Ada Fincastle becomes a serial heroine, a soap-opera queen.

Consider the list of her wrongs. Ralph McBride is wrested from her by an unscrupulous girl friend and returns, a married man, to make her pregnant. Ironside spits at her, and her grandmother dies of the disgrace. Ralph eventually marries her, but war neuroses have made him moody and unfaithful, and in Queenborough, during the depression, they are reduced to desperate want. Ralph, out driving with the girl next door, is nearly paralyzed in an automobile accident. Yet Ada is always superb; her vein of iron sees her through. The reader must take it on faith. One does not see her, as one sees Dorinda in *Barren Ground*, working on her farm, milking cows, supervising the help, purchasing new fields. Even in *Life and Gabriella* one sees what Gabriella does in her shop, so that one has a sense of the therapy which she applies to her sorrow. But Ada relies simply on her inheritance of character.

The book ends on a harsh note of denunciation of the formlessness and aimlessness of life in the 1930's, a theme that is picked up and enlarged upon in Miss Glasgow's final novel, *In This Our Life* (1941), where the amoralism in which she believed Richmond to have been engulfed seems to have affected not only the young but the old and — one almost suspects — the author herself. For how else can one explain Asa Timberlake?

At first blush he seems in the tradition of Honeywell, Littlepage, and Archbald, those elderly, nostalgic gentlemen who have missed the thrills as well as the substance of life, and like them he has his creator's sympathy. "For the sake of a past tradition he had spent nearly thirty years doing things that he hated and not doing things that he liked; and at the end of that long self-discipline, when he was too old to begin over again, he had seen his code of conduct flatten out and shrivel up as utterly as a balloon that is pricked." But *was* it self-discipline? Asa's life has simply gone by default; he is that commonest of American fictional heroes, the husband dominated by a strong-minded hypochondriac wife. But Asa has none of the dignity of his predecessors in the Queenborough trilogy; he is plotting, with the author's apparent approval, a weak man's escape. As soon as his wife shall have inherited the fortune of a rich uncle, he will quietly decamp with the widow of an old friend. Surely he is as bad as the young folk.

Well, not quite, for they are monsters. Roy, the heroine, and Peter have married with the understanding that either may have back her or his liberty on request. There is, of course, the similar bargain between the young couple in Mrs. Wharton's equally disapproving novel, *The Glimpses of the Moon*. Roy's sister, Stanley, ditches her fiancé, Craig, in order to take Peter from Roy, and then, having driven Peter to suicide, she returns to rob her sister a second time, of Craig with whom poor Roy has been consoling herself. During all of these goings-on the four characters, like Asa, are saturated with self-pity. One feels that Miss Glasgow's conviction that men are doomed to weakness and that women can rise above their destiny of betrayal only by stoicism has now reached the pitch of an obsession. Yet she works her plot around the gravely offered thesis that love is vital to the young because it is "the only reality left," though it cannot save them because they treat each other "as if they were careless fellow-travellers, to be picked up and dropped, either by accident or by design, on a very brief journey." But that is not necessarily one's own experience of America in 1938 when the action of the novel takes place.

There are, however, moments. There are always moments, even in the least estimable of Ellen Glasgow's books. When Stanley tries to put the blame of her hit-and-run accident on a Negro boy, and the family prepare to back her up, the novel suddenly soars in stature. Here, at last, is a problem that is real and competently handled, the only time, too, in nineteen novels where Miss Glasgow faces, however briefly, what the South has done to its colored people. And Uncle William Fitzroy, the tycoon whose millions have vulgarized him, despite his genteel background, into the likeness of a noisy parvenu, the forerunner of "Big Daddy" in *Cat on a Hot Tin Roof*, seems to bring Tennessee Williams and Ellen Glasgow into brief but entrancing partnership.

Mention should be made of Miss Glasgow's twelve short stories recently assembled in a volume by Richard K. Meeker. It was not a medium that she much liked or in which she enjoyed much success. She was a discursive writer and needed space to appear to her best advantage. Almost half of the stories deal, as might be anticipated, with the struggle of women with men who are not worthy of them, the theme that underlies so much of her "social history" of the South. As Mr. Meeker amusingly sums it up: "Her typical plot sequence runs: girl meets boy; girl is taken advantage of by boy; then girl learns to get along without boy, or girl gets back at boy."

Best of the tales are four ghost stories, all told in the first person, a method adopted in only one of her novels, but a useful one in helping the reader suspend his disbelief. "Dare's Gift" and "Whispering Leaves" are most effective because of their atmosphere of old Virginia mansions which she knew so well how to evoke; but because in her earlier writing she had no interest in keeping things back, because she seemed, on the contrary, to have almost a compulsion to let her reader know what was on her mind at each moment, she had to remain an amateur in the fiction of the supernatural.

In 1954, nine years after Ellen Glasgow's death of heart disease, her literary executors published under the title *The Woman Within* the memoirs that had been confided to their discretion. There were those who were distressed by this posthumous revelation of the author's self-pity and vanity and who claimed that the memoirs gave a wrong impression of a woman who had always seemed in life so gay and bright and full of sympathy for others. But so long as one bears in mind that this is only Ellen Glasgow as Ellen Glasgow saw her, *The Woman Within* is filled with valuable insights.

It also contains some of her best writing. The pages about

"Harold S——," the snob and name-dropper, are as good as anything in *The Romantic Comedians*, and the irony is supplied by the memoirist herself who was in love with the man she despised. How could one get a better glimpse of an author at work than in her description of her meeting with Harold: "I observed him for an instant over my cocktail, wondering whether he could be used effectively in a comedy of manners. My curiosity flagged. What on earth could I find to talk about to a person like that?" What indeed? Yet the association that began that night was to last twenty-one years. So we see the novelist looking for a story and finding one — as ironical as any she wrote — happening to herself. Why, she asks herself in despair, was Harold fated to meet every crisis with a spectacular gesture? "Afterwards, when I read in the 'Life Story' of a Balkan Queen, that, as she said farewell to a Southern Colonel, he had fallen on his knees before her and kissed the hem of her skirt, I recognized the last act of chivalry. So Harold had parted from me when he sailed for the Balkans."

The most valuable thing in the memoirs, however, is the picture of a woman's dedication to her art. From the beginning she had wanted to be a writer above everything, and not just a writer, but specifically a novelist. After the publication of her first book she realized that she needed a steadier control over her ideas and material, a philosophy of fiction, a prose style so pure and flexible that it could bend without breaking. From Maupassant she gained a great deal, but not until, by accident, she happened to read *War and Peace* did she know what she needed. "Life must use art; art must use life. . . . One might select realities, but one could not impose on Reality. Not if one were honest in one's interpretation, not if one possessed artistic integrity. For truth to art became in the end simple fidelity to one's own inner vision." She summed up her artistic credo as follows: "I had always wished to escape from the particular into the general, from the provincial into the universal. Never from my earliest blind gropings after truth in art and truth in life had I felt an impulse to write of a single locality or of regional characteristics. From the beginning I had resolved to write of the South, not, in elegy, as a conquered province, but, vitally, as a part of the larger world. Tolstoy made me see clearly what I had realized dimly, that the ordinary is simply the universal observed from the surface, that the direct approach to reality is not without, but within."

It puts one off a bit that Ellen Glasgow struck, again and again, so high a note for herself. As she conceived of her personal sufferings as more intense than anyone else's, so did she conceive of herself as a novelist on a Tolstoian scale. She did not hesitate, in the preface to *Barren Ground*, to nominate it as the one of her books best qualified for immortality, and in her memoirs she described it further, together with the Queenborough trilogy and *Vein of Iron*, as representing "not only the best that was in me, but some of the best work that has been done in American fiction." In her personal philosophy, and despite a sensitive mind that "would always remain an exile on earth," she believed that she had found a code of living that was sufficient for life or for death. And in her later years she loved to play the queen in the New York publishing world, dangling the possibility of her largesse, half in jest, half in earnest, before the different editors who bid for her books. John Farrar relates that when she made her ultimate decision to go to Alfred Harcourt, the latter went down on his knees before her in her hotel suite like Harold S——— before Marie of Romania. But one can see through the boasting and the jesting, with its aspect of essentially southern horseplay, to her never joking resolution and determination to be a great novelist. One can look back at the young Ellen Glasgow like the young Victoria (to evoke another queen), affirming solemnly her will to be good.

The advantages that she brought to her task and ambition were indeed considerable. Out of her wide reading she selected the mightiest and probably the best models to guide her in her re-creation of the Virginia scene. She used Hardy as her master in rustic atmosphere, George Eliot as her guide in morality, Maupassant for plot, and Tolstoy for everything. She had the richest source material that any author could wish, consisting simply of a whole state and its whole history, a state, too, that occupies the center of our eastern geography and of our history and that not coincidentally has produced more Presidents than any other. And the social range among

Miss Glasgow's characters is far greater than that of most twentieth-century novelists, suggesting that of such Victorians as Trollope, Dickens, Elizabeth Gaskell, and, again, George Eliot.

She not only considered every social group, but she covered wide varieties within each. In the top ranks of the old hierarchy she showed aristocrats in their glory, such as Major Lightfoot, and aristocrats in their decay, such as Beverly Brooke (in *The Ancient Law*). She showed them turning to the new world of business and dominating it, such as General Bolingbroke, and turning to the same world to be dominated and ultimately vulgarized by it, such as William Fitzroy. She showed aristocrats surviving into our own time, such as Judge Honeywell and Virginius Littlepage, having made the necessary adjustments and compromises, respectable, prosperous, but curiously unsatisfied, and she showed aristocrats like Asa Timberlake, who have been beaten into mediocrity and have failed in life without even the consolation and romance of a picturesque decay. Among the women of this world she created such magnificent anachronisms as Mrs. Blake, such noble, docile, and submissive wives as Virginia Pendleton, such apparently submissive but actually dominating mothers as Mrs. Gay, and such a reconstructed success in the North as Gabriella Carr.

In the middle ranks we find the rising businessman, Ben Starr, the risen politician, Gideon Vetch, the corrupt overseer, Bill Fletcher, the poor philosopher, John Fincastle, the "yeoman" farmers, Dorinda Oakley and Nathan Pedlar, the thriving miller, Abel Revercomb, and, among the lower orders, the "poor white" Burr family, the Starrs from whose midst Ben rises, the victims of the Richmond slums whom Stephen Culpeper is made to visit, the village prostitute and her idiot son in *Vein of Iron*, and, of course, all the Negro servants. Despite what has already been said about the limitations of Miss Glasgow's characterization of Negroes, the servants in her novels are absolutely alive and convincing. In at least one instance, that of the maid and companion to Dorinda in *Barren Ground*, the characterization is as successful as of any of the author's other women.

Miss Glasgow had the same range in scenery that she had in human beings, and she could make the transfer without difficulty from the grim mountains and valleys of *Vein of Iron* to the interminable fields of broomsedge in *Barren Ground* and thence to the comfortable mansions of Richmond and to the smaller gentility of Petersburg and Williamsburg. Highly individual in American letters is her ability to pass with equal authority from country to city, from rusticity to sophistication, from the tobacco field to the drawing room, from irony to tragedy.

Yet for all her gifts and advantages she does not stand in the very first rank of American novelists. She was unable sufficiently to pull the tapestry of fiction over her personal grievances and approbations. The latter are always peeping out at the oddest times and in the oddest places. It is strange that a novelist of such cultivation and such fecundity and one who was also such a student of her craft should not have seen her own glaring faults. How is it possible that the woman who could imagine the brilliant repartee of Edmonia Bredalbane, which annihilates every vestige of pretentiousness in Queenborough, should not have torn up the dreary sermon that is called *The Builders*? How could the author of prose which conveys all the beauty and mystery of the desolate countryside in *Barren Ground* have written the tired purple passages in earlier novels which describe the animal charm of handsome men and women in terms that might have been lifted from the very women's magazines that she so violently despised? How, moreover, could she have failed to see that her own bitterness on the subject of men was reflected in her heroines to the point of warping the whole picture of their lives? The mystery of Ellen Glasgow is not so much how she could be so good a writer as how she could on occasion be so bad a one.

Like Edith Wharton, she will be remembered for her women, not her men. The course of her heroes is a curious one. They start, romantically enough, as men of fierce ideals and raging passions, Byronic in their excesses, impatient of injustice and burning to remake the world. Akershem and Burr are men of the people; the lowness of their origin contributes to their strength, their violence, and their sex appeal. They are a bit lurid, but there will come a time in Miss Glasgow's fiction when we would be glad enough to see them again. With Dan Montjoy in *The Battle-Ground* she inaugurated a period of more respectable, conventional heroes. He is followed by Christopher Blake, Ben Starr, and Abel Revercomb, all of them men of considerable strength and power. But in *Virginia* the weak, selfish, deserting male makes his appearance, and he is to stay through to the end of her fiction. Oliver Treadwell, George Fowler, Jason Greylock, George Birdsong, Peter Kingsmill, Martin Welding, Ralph McBride, and Craig Fleming are all faithless to good women who love them and are all faithless more from the weakness of their characters than the force of their passions. What is most appalling in Miss Glasgow's indictment is that the only ground of redemption that she can find in those of them whom she regards as redeemable, i.e. the last three of the list, is a groveling, lachrymose self-pity. Listen to Martin Welding as his father-in-law interrogates him about the unhappiness of his marriage to Mary Victoria:

"Why don't you tell me about it and let me help you?" the older man asked with all the sympathy that he could summon.

The merest flicker of gratitude shone in the sullen misery of Martin's look. "The trouble is that I have come to the end of my rope. I am wondering how much longer I shall be able to stand it."

"Stand what, my boy?"

"Stand the whole thing. Stand life, stand marriage, stand women."

Mr. Littlepage frowned. "But this isn't normal," he said sternly. "This isn't rational."

"Well, what am I to do?"

"You should see a physician."

"I've seen dozens of them since I met Mary Victoria."

"And what do they say?"

"That I'm not normal, I'm not rational."

"Then, it seems to me, you will have to believe it."

"I do believe it, but that doesn't make it easier. I am still that way no matter what I believe."

The men would not matter so much if they were not taken quite so seriously by the women. Lawrence Selden in Edith Wharton's *The House of Mirth* is a passive spectator hero, but Lily Bart suffers little enough from his preference for the sidelines. Miss Glasgow's heroines, on the other hand, are devastated by her worthless men, and it is just here that her fiction is pulled most seriously out of line. Acceptance of Dorinda Oakley and Gabriella Carr as the towers of strength that they must be to accomplish what they do is difficult to reconcile with the long, tortured passages in which they dwell with the lovingness of hypochondriacs upon their grief. One wonders if their kind of women would not have thrown off disappointment and disillusionment with more dispatch and if Miss Glasgow was not attributing her own sensitivity to natures that had, by definition, to possess tougher fibers. In the final novel the question is reduced to absurdity by Roy Timberlake who succeeds in being abandoned by *two* men and suffers equally at the hands of each.

For all her faults, however, it is hard to get away from the fact that without Ellen Glasgow there would be a great gap in our fiction, particularly where it concerns the South. She was determined to reproduce the South as it was, and although we are conscious today of things added and things omitted, we search in vain for any contemporary or predecessor of hers who even approached her accomplishment. Furthermore, it is astonishing to consider how different in style and mood were her three principal works. *Virginia* might not be worthy of Flaubert, but one suspects that Zola would not have disowned it, nor would Hardy have been ashamed of *Barren Ground*. And any novelist of manners would have been delighted to have produced *The Romantic Comedians*.

Frederick P. W. McDowell has astutely pointed out that Ellen Glasgow's accomplishments and limitations as a writer are best suggested in her own judgment of another southern writer, Edgar Allan Poe: "Poe is, to a large extent, a distillation of the Southern. The formalism of his tone, the classical element in his poetry and in many of his stories, the drift toward rhetoric, the aloof and elusive intensity, — all these qualities are Southern. And in his more serious faults of overwriting, sentimental exaggeration, and lapses, now and then, into a pompous or florid style, he belongs to his epoch and even more to his South."

When Ellen Glasgow began her career, there was almost no serious literature in the South. The pioneer element in her work today is obscured by the fact that the romantic school of southern fiction against which she reacted not only has disappeared but has hardly left a trace. Similarly, the modern school has gone so far beyond her in exploration of the freakish and the decadent that she seems as mild in comparison as Mary Johnston or Amélie Rives. She herself enlarged the distance between her work and that of the southern novelists who were becoming popular in her later years by deriding them. "One may admit that the Southern States have more than an equal share of degeneracy and deterioration; but the multitude of half-wits, and whole idiots, and nymphomaniacs, and paranoiacs, and rakehells in general, that populate the modern literary South could flourish nowhere but in the weird pages of melodrama." Yet she herself is the bridge, and the necessary bridge, between the world of Thomas Nelson Page and the world of William Faulkner, Katherine Anne Porter, Eudora Welty, and Tennessee Williams.

She will probably not be remembered as the historian of Virginia that she wished to be. This ambition may have been too great for the fiction that she produced. Only four of her nineteen novels, *Virginia, Barren Ground, The Romantic Comedians,* and *The Sheltered Life,* have won more than a temporary place in American letters. But her picture of the South emerging from defeat and reconstruction with all its old legends intact and all its old energy preserved and managing to adapt itself, almost without admitting it, to the industrial exigencies of a new age — like the Bourbons in that it had forgotten nothing, but unlike them in that it had learned a lot — is one that has passed into our sense of American history.

WILLA CATHER

WILLA CATHER was born in 1873 in Back Creek Valley, near Winchester, in the northern neck of Virginia, where the Cathers, reputedly of Irish origin, had been farmers since the eighteenth century. The country was hilly, rocky, and sandy, little fitted for the "peculiar institution," and few of the farmers, whose main business was raising sheep, owned slaves. Some of the Cathers had even been Union sympathizers in the war. They were substantial people, but not of the antebellum upper class; Willa's branch of the family lived in a plain, red brick, three-story house that gave an impression to her biographer, E. K. Brown, of "indestructible solidity." He goes on to speculate that the qualities of continuity and stability which she was later so much to cherish might have owed some of their hold to the conservatism of this rural Virginia of her first nine years. She never used it, at any rate, as subject material until the end of her life, when she set it in an era antecedent to her own recollections. *Sapphira and the Slave Girl* treats the northern Virginia of Willa Cather's grandmother's day.

She was the first born of seven. Her father, Charles Cather, was a popular, courteous, fair-minded gentleman, perhaps a bit deficient in energy, and it was her mother, Virginia Boak Cather, a handsome, vigorous, imperious woman, who controlled the family.

The move to Nebraska in Willa's tenth year was occasioned osten-
sibly by the drier air (the Cathers as a family were thought to be
prone to tuberculosis), but also, one suspects, by the hope for
greater prosperity with better soil. Webster County in 1884 was
still frontier land. For a year Charles Cather farmed, making corn-
fields where for centuries there had been nothing but flat ground
stretching to the horizon and high, rough, shaggy red grass, the
color of wine stains. Then, to the regret of the young Willa, who
was already under the spell of the countryside, he moved into the
little town of Red Cloud, which his daughter's readers were to
know under many names ("Sweet Water," "Frankfort," "Haver-
ford," "Moonstone," "Black Hawk," "Hanover"), and set up a
mortgage loan business. All of his large family, including his moth-
er-in-law, had to squeeze into a small white frame house, one and
a half stories high, which was to be Willa's home until she left
Nebraska for the East.

The change in the Cathers' social position from their Virginia
days was aptly described, more than four decades later, in "Old
Mrs. Harris," one of three stories in *Obscure Destinies*: "Mrs. Harris was no longer living in a feudal society, where there were plenty
of landless people glad to render service to the more fortunate, but
in a snappy little Western democracy, where every man was as
good as his neighbour and out to prove it."

Willa, an unconventional child, who dressed in a boyish manner
and took an unfeminine, precocious interest in surgery and even
embalming (at fourteen her "idea of perfect happiness" was am-
putating limbs), learned at an early age from other children and
their parents the pain that can be inflicted by that terrible weapon
of the "bitter, dead little Western town": the tongue. Life did not
really begin until her enrollment at the University of Nebraska, and
even there the advent must have seemed inauspicious. A fellow student recalled her arrival in class. The door opened; a head appeared
with short hair and a straw hat, and a deep voice inquired if this
were the Greek class. Somebody nodded, and the door opened wider
to admit — a girl. Shouts of laughter. Poor Willa Cather! But one
imagines they did not laugh long. Ravenously, she tore at all the

college had to offer, distinguishing herself in linguistic and literary courses; she discovered music, Flaubert, and Robert Louis Stevenson; she edited the *Hesperean* and contributed drama criticism to the *State Journal*. She also dropped her masculine affectations, and made many friends. It was a busy and fruitful time.

Graduation was followed by an anticlimactic year in Red Cloud, helping her father with land titles and mortgages, but on a visit to Lincoln she met a Pittsburgh businessman who offered her the editorship of a small family magazine, the *Home Monthly*, that he was planning to start. For a decade, from her twenty-third to her thirty-third years, Willa Cather lived in Pittsburgh. She left the *Home Monthly* to become a newswriter and drama critic for the *Daily Leader* and then quit the newspaper business altogether to become a teacher of English in the high schools. She led a rather dreary, drudging existence in copy rooms, school buildings, and boardinghouses, relieved only by passionately enjoyed concerts and plays, until in 1901 she formed a close friendship with Isabelle McClung, the daughter of a conservative and affluent family, and went to live with them in a large, stately house on Murray Hill Avenue. This meant not only release from financial pressure; it meant trips to Europe and time to write. As Elizabeth Shepley Sergeant put it, in her excellent *Willa Cather: A Memoir*: "Willa had more natural affinity for *la vie de famille* than for *la vie de bohème*: after her long bout with uncongenial surroundings she enjoyed the protected, delicately nurtured life of the well-to-do. At the McClungs' her personal liberties were respected. Isabelle McClung, the daughter of the house, beautiful, intelligent and identified with the arts herself, rather than with the social round of the rich young lady, had read Willa Cather's work in the newspaper, and had met her in the dressing room of an actress. If not herself an artist, Isabelle, as a patroness of the arts, could help to create one."

Willa Cather now published her first two volumes: *April Twilights* (1903), a collection of only moderately competent little poems, with here and there a faintly embarrassing echo of A. E. Housman, and *The Troll Garden* (1905), a medley of Jamesian stories of artists and their problems, the best of which were later included in *Youth and the Bright Medusa*. Probably the most important thing about *The Troll Garden* was that it impressed S. S. McClure sufficiently to induce him to go to Pittsburgh to offer Miss Cather a job on his magazine. She accepted at once and moved to New York which was to be her home, or at least the home port of her many travels, for the rest of her life.

Willa Cather admired S. S. McClure with the same deep admiration that she accorded the pioneers who had opened up the West. From 1908 until 1912 she was his managing editor and near slave, writing fiction as well as nonfiction, interviewing and researching, working at the nerve center of a machine of nerves. It must have been a happy period, for all her misgivings about the waste of artistic energy, for we have this picture of her from Miss Sergeant, garnered on the latter's first interview: "Her eyes were sailor-blue, her cheeks were rosy, her hair was red-brown, parted in the middle like a child's. As she shook hands, I felt the freshness and brusqueness, too, of an ocean breeze. Her boyish, enthusiastic manner was disarming, and as she led me through the jostle of the outer office, I was affected by the resonance of her Western voice, and by the informality of her clothes — it was as if she rebelled against urban conformities."

But as soon as Miss Cather started on business the "ballad lady" was gone, and Miss Sergeant felt the impact beneath her editorial mask of "crude oil, red earth, elemental strength and resoluteness." Later, as good friends, Miss Sergeant discovered that Willa Cather had many interests outside her work, that she was a gourmet, an opera and theater addict, an eager tourist, both abroad and at home, and that her favorite Saturday afternoon diversion was riding up Fifth Avenue on the top of an open bus from which she would identify all visible landmarks, including the French châteaux of the Vanderbilts and Astors. Willa Cather did not laugh, however, at the swagger of the latter. Financial success she was always to equate with the winning of the West.

When she went to Boston in 1908 to study the career of Mary Baker Eddy in the course of her work on a series of articles appearing in *McClure's*, she met Sarah Orne Jewett, and they immediately became friends. The spinster authoress from South Berwick, Maine, must have represented to the younger woman much of what she most deeply wanted for herself. Miss Jewett lived in a large, still beautiful house in the center of the world that she had achieved her fame by describing. She was the uninterrupted artist, without distractions except of her own choosing, and the rich result of this in her quiet, perfect stories, uncluttered by the elaborate plotting of current fiction and redolent of the air and coast of Maine, the novel "démeublé" as Miss Cather was later to put it, might have been the model for what she herself was one day to do for Nebraska. Miss Jewett was then in the last year of her life, and she wrote Willa Cather a letter that was a kind of testament, urging her to give up journalism and devote herself entirely to fiction. Willa had now gathered, she pointed out, her capital of subject matter — her Nebraska life, her childhood Virginia, her intimate knowledge of the journalist's world — and the time had come to be a "looker-on" and not a participant: ". . . if you don't keep and guard and mature your force, and above all, have time and quiet to perfect your work, you will be writing things not much better than you did five years ago. . . . your vivid, exciting companionship in the office must not be your audience, you must find your own quiet centre of life, and write from that to . . . the human heart . . . Otherwise what might be strength in a writer is only crudeness, and what might be insight is only observation; sentiment falls to sentimentality — you can write about life, but never write life itself. . . . To work in silence and with all one's heart, that is the writer's lot; he is the only artist who must be a solitary, and yet needs the widest outlook upon the world."

It took four years for this seed of wisdom to ripen, but Willa Cather did not possess Miss Jewett's financial independence, and she was never willing to live in a garret. It was four years later, in 1912, when she was on the brink of forty, before she felt ready to take the great step, and then she resigned from *McClure's* and took a long holiday trip to the American Southwest. The landscape of Arizona and New Mexico, the Indians and Mexicans, the survivals of Aztec beauty were a shock and a great delight to her. She had discovered for the first time an American past that had significance to her, and she was to make great use of it.

Returning to New York, she and her friend Edith Lewis (Isabelle McClung had married) rented a seven-room, high-ceilinged apartment in a wide, brick, five-story house at No. 5 Bank Street in Greenwich Village which was to be home for twenty-five years. Miss Lewis wrote of it: "After we had made the apartment fairly comfortable, we gave no more thought to acquiring new things, or getting better ones than those we had. What money we had we preferred to spend on flowers, music, and entertaining our friends." Now Willa Cather's best years began: she was no longer harried and pressed, and the fatigue and depression of later years had not yet appeared. From this point her biography becomes her books.

Alexander's Bridge (1912) was written before her retirement from *McClure's*, but its publication was roughly simultaneous. The setting is international and certainly in no way suggests the later Nebraska stories; the novel might have been written by a conscientious Jamesian disciple who had never been west of Massachusetts. Bartley Alexander, the protagonist, keeps his Canadian wife in Boston and his Irish mistress in London. He is represented to the reader as being a great man and a great engineer and is likened to the bridges which he has constructed. In the end he dies with his laborers in the river after the collapse of his most ambitious span. Both Alexander and his bridge, it appears, suffer from a hidden defect. "When a great man dies in his prime there is no surgeon who can say whether he did well; whether or not the future was his, as it seemed to be. The mind that society had come to regard as a powerful and reliable machine, dedicated to its service, may for a long time have been sick within itself and bent upon its own destruction."

Of course, today we would assume that Alexander's subconscious had plotted the overstrain of the bridge to bring about his death, but that was not the way Miss Cather's imagination worked in 1912. What then did she mean by Alexander's sickness? As the plot of the novel turns on his adultery, it is tempting to try to identify it with his infatuation for his mistress, but this will not fit. Not only is Hilda portrayed as a splendid, brave woman who was in love with Alexander before he met his wife, while Winifred is shown as an unappealing though vaguely noble individual, but Willa Cather goes out of her way to make it clear that Alexander does not really love his mistress. He maintains to himself that only his energy, the energy of youth, is concerned with Hilda.

That, then, is the clue to the arcane tragedy: Alexander has sinned by letting himself fall from an early native grandeur, by "letting himself go with the crowd." He has allowed his career to build him into a person swallowed up in details, and he wonders what the young man he once was would have become in a less cluttered existence. It is this habit of speculation, of nostalgia, that causes to be born in him again a counterpart of that young man, an "energy," which cannot be contained by the actual Bartley Alexander and which destroys him. Alexander, having gone "with the crowd," must die with the crowd, pulled down in the river while swimming to safety by the panic-crazed laborers. But why, then, does the bridge fall? Is it implied that it has been faultily designed because of Alexander's failing powers? Or is it merely a convenient symbol of his own disintegration, if we accept the fact (nowhere really apparent) that he *is* disintegrating?

This short novel would not be remembered today without the fame of its successors, but it has a beautifully sustained unity of mood, and its prose is clear and strong. Willa Cather herself became impatient with its artificiality, its contrived plot, and she ultimately rejected the whole business of the "well-made" novel. As she put it in a preface to a later issue of *Alexander's Bridge*, a writer comes of age when he ceases to draw his material from what he has discovered and begins to use what all the while has been lying at the bottom of his consciousness.

Ferris Greenslet, of Houghton Mifflin, had persuaded his associates to publish *Alexander's Bridge*, stressing "the spiritual sense of life that informs it," but when he read the manuscript of *O Pioneers!* (1913) he was able exultantly to assure them that it should "definitely establish the author as a novelist of the first rank." Yet for many today her second novel's interest is largely as an advance study

WILLA CATHER 99

for *My Ántonia*. So much has been written since 1913 about the glory of the American soil and the American farmer that her book's hymn-like quality, instead of striking us as freshly as it did its readers in 1913, seems overwritten and, at worst, banal. Alexandra Bergson, the superwoman, the virgin goddess who conquers the recalcitrant soil, a big, calm, strong, earthy Ceres, has none of the appeal of Ántonia Shimerda. When her dying father instructs his sons to obey her in all that concerns the land, she might be Joan of Arc taking command of the armies of France. The good people are too crudely identified with the good earth, as in the passage describing Emil Bergson: "There is something frank and joyous and young in the open face of the country. . . . He was a splendid figure of a boy, tall and straight as a young pine tree, with a handsome head, and stormy gray eyes."

Yet for all its approach to sentimentality *O Pioneers!* is the work of a major novelist who has at last discovered her form and her subject. One would never suspect that it was written by the author of *Alexander's Bridge*. At its best it is almost as good as Willa Cather was ever to write. Its theme is the conquest of virgin soil by pioneers. "The history of every country begins in the heart of a man or a woman." The land, which in the opening chapters seems "to overwhelm the little beginnings of human society that struggled in its sombre wastes," is tamed by man in the person of Alexandra. Once she has asserted her control, the whole countryside is bathed in a calm green fertility, and the brown earth yields itself eagerly to the plow and rolls away from the shear without even dimming the brightness of the metal, exuding "a soft, deep sigh of happiness." In the end the land is apostrophized as fortunate to receive one day to its bosom a heart like Alexandra's and to be able to give back that heart again in yellow wheat and corn and the shining eyes of youth. The picture is overcolored, but it is still a memorable picture.

It would have been better had Miss Cather not added a little tale to show how even a good man, sprung, so to speak, from good soil, like Alexandra's younger brother, Emil, can be destroyed by the innate perversity of his species. There are good men and bad men, like good soil and bad soil, and there seems to be little question of fault or even of choice in which they are. Marie Shabata is "too beautiful, too full of life and love"; it is "through no fault" of her own that she spreads ruin around her. But Willa Cather destroys her own argument by representing Marie as a sexy, unprincipled flirt who abandons herself recklessly to Emil in her husband's orchard under circumstances that make detection and murder almost necessary consequences. The whole episode of the Shabatas and Alexandra's later visit to the crazed husband in prison seem basically irrelevant to the story of the land.

Elizabeth Sergeant records that Willa Cather agreed with her criticism that *O Pioneers!* lacked a sharp skeleton, but argued that the Nebraskan prairies (which presumably dictated her structure) had no sculptured lines or features. But had she let her situation work itself out, as she claimed she was trying to do, she would never have forced upon it the Shabata triangle, and the book would not have lost its unity of mood. The only advantage of the murder and aftermath is that they diminish the interest in Alexandra and hence the faint embarrassment in her late-blooming romance with the younger Carl Linstrum. When Ellen Glasgow, a dozen years later, wrote *Barren Ground*, about another old maid who conquered the soil, she also gave her protagonist a husband in middle age, but she added the interesting and perhaps significant detail that the marriage was never consummated.

Willa Cather said of her next and longest novel, *The Song of the Lark* (1915), that it should have ended with Thea Kronborg's first surmountal of her difficulties, that having escaped to Chicago from the stultification of Moonstone, where a concert or operatic career was inconceivable, and having discovered at last that her instrument was not the piano but the voice, she should have been left, one foot firmly set on the first rung of her long ladder. Perhaps. Certainly the book would have been more of a unit, with its superb picture of a dauntless soul (based, no doubt, with a touch of self-pity, on the author) caught in a small town dead to the smallest aspiration or the timidest dream, who with the aid of a $600 insurance policy, paid on the death of a young freight train conductor who selflessly loved her, escapes at last to Chicago and music school and hope.

It is a sorry but effective indictment of the other side of the coin of the American frontier: the hot little dried-up towns, unredeemed by the prairie breeze, that had neither the culture of the eastern seaboard nor the philosophy that comes from struggle with the soil.

Yet one can see no real reason why Thea should be left in Chicago. The trouble with the second part of the novel, which tells of her triumph as an opera star, is not, as Miss Cather thought, that a great singer becomes less interesting as she loses herself in her art, but that *she* loses Thea Kronborg. The picture of an artist's self-immolation, despite what she says, *could* be intensely interesting. Elizabeth Sergeant's picture of Willa Cather herself as an older woman and successful writer, preoccupied, opinionated, and remote, is proof of that. No, the trouble with the second part of *The Song of the Lark* is that it ceases to be a book about an opera singer and becomes a book about opera. And opera lovers, even Miss Cather, have a tendency to be fulsome in writing of their love. There are bits of *The Song of the Lark* that sound like intermission notes on a Saturday afternoon broadcast of the Metropolitan Opera.

Even the plot in the second half becomes hurried and blurred. The romance with the rich, handsome Fred Ottenburg — a *Jane Eyre* tale of planned bigamy — is slid over, for Thea seems little affected either by his love or by his fraud. Its real function seems to be to introduce the scenic grandeur of the Southwest — which Willa Cather always used to great effect — when Thea and Fred take their trip to Arizona. We then leap over ten years to see Thea making a hit as Sieglinde in a scene reminiscent of the climax of one of those pedestrian cinematic biographies of musical artists popular in the 1930's. The trouble is that one does not see Thea as an opera star at all. She is too noble, too dedicated, too pure. She has no men, no temperament, no ego. She cares more about being Sieglinde than being applauded as Sieglinde. She is too much an artist, too little a woman; too much a musical instrument, too little a diva.

Willa Cather made no secret of having modeled her, at least in part, on Olive Fremstad, the beautiful Swedish opera star (raised in Minnesota) who retired from the Metropolitan at the peak of her powers at the age of forty-two. She knew Fremstad and admired her passionately, and the latter, in reading *The Song of the Lark*, said that she hardly knew where Kronborg stopped and Fremstad began. If Miss Cather's heroine is really a good likeness of the Swedish singer, then perhaps she would have done better to write a biography instead of a novel, for fiction should deal in universals rather than particulars. But one may doubt the likeness. One suspects that the young Thea has more of Willa Cather in her than anyone else and that Thea, the great star, is Willa Cather's fantasy of herself, with Fremstad's looks and Fremstad's voice, singing Sieglinde. We all have such fantasies, but they are not the soil from which great novels spring. They spring, and were in Willa Cather's case about to spring, from deeper sources. "Life began for me," she wrote, "when I ceased to admire and began to remember."

In 1916, on a trip back to Red Cloud, she drove out to a farm on the Divide to visit a Bohemian woman, Anna Pavelka, whom she had known and admired in her youth, and found her serene and happy, surrounded by many children. As E. K. Brown put it: "It seemed to her that this woman's story ran very close to the central stream of life in Red Cloud and on the Divide, that she stood for the triumph of what was vigorous, sound, and beautiful in a region where these qualities so often seemed to suffer repression or defeat." Even before her return to New York Willa Cather had started *My Ántonia* (1918).

The introduction to it, read in conjunction with the later preface to the reissue of *Alexander's Bridge*, presents a fascinating question to those who care how a novel is constructed. Jim Burden, who is to be the "I" of the story, tells another "I" — a character of undetermined sex who has grown up in the same Nebraska town with him — how he comes to write his memories of Ántonia. We learn from this prefatory "I" that Jim's wife is a snobbish society woman, a patroness of artists "of advanced ideas and mediocre ability," and that Jim, a successful railroad lawyer, lives largely apart from her, traveling back and forth across the great country which the rails of his road span. Success, however, has not destroyed his romantic disposition or his nostalgia for his Nebraskan boyhood which, both to him and to "I," is dominated by the memory of a Bohemian girl, Ántonia Shimerda. "More than any other person we remembered, this girl seemed to mean to us the country, the conditions, the whole adventure of our childhood." Jim later sends "I" the narrative that he has written, which is called *My Ántonia*. He insists that he has written it down as it has come to his mind and that "it hasn't any form."

Indeed, it seems not to have. Certainly without either the title of the novel or the introduction one would never on a first reading (at least until near the end) gather that it is primarily about Ántonia. The first part, "The Shimerdas," is much more concerned with Jim Burden's impressions of his grandparents' farm in Nebraska than with the Shimerdas, a poor Bohemian family in the neighborhood who are fighting a losing battle with a ragged farm for which they have paid too much. The narrative is interrupted by a bloodcurdling tale of a young bride and groom in Russia being thrown from a sled to halt pursuing wolves. It is a brilliant and horrifying little piece that has nothing to do with anything else in the novel. The part ends with the tragic suicide of old Mr. Shimerda, the defeated immigrant, in which Ántonia plays only a small part.

In the next part, "The Hired Girls," the Burdens and Jim move into the town of Black Hawk (as the Cathers moved to Red Cloud), and Ántonia leaves her family's farm to become a domestic servant at the Harlings', down the street. Here we begin to see her more clearly, particularly when she throws up her job rather than give up the weekly dances where Mrs. Harling feels that she meets bad company. "A girl like me has got to take her good times when she can." Then comes the episode of Mr. Cutter's attempted rape of Ántonia which tells us far more of him than of her. Mr. Cutter and his wife are a bizarre, Dickensian couple; he eventually murders her and kills himself, a provable few minutes later, to ensure that her next-of-kin will not share in his estate. The narrative then shifts altogether to Lena Lingard and Tiny Soderball, the hired girls who make good, one as a dressmaker and the other as a gold miner, and we learn only indirectly from the Widow Steavens that Ántonia has been seduced by Larry Donovan and abandoned with an illegitimate child. These most important events are seen fleetingly and at second hand. Not until the very end do we see Ántonia in the center of the stage when Jim Burden calls on her, many years later, to find her contentedly married to a poor but kindly farmer, Anton Cuzak, and surrounded by a big family of beautiful children, a far more fitting symbol of the fertile land than the old-maid Alexandra Bergson.

Jim Burden's statement that his narrative is without shape receives an echo in Willa Cather's preface to the reissue of *Alexander's Bridge*. After stating that a writer's best material is in himself, already molded, she proceeds thus: "If he tries to meddle with its vague outline, to twist it into some categorical shape, above all if he tries to adapt or modify its mood, he destroys its value. In working with this material he finds that he need have little to do with literary devices; he comes to depend more and more on something else — the thing by which our feet find the road home on a dark night, accounting of themselves for roots and stones which we had never noticed by day."

This passage comes very near to being her literary credo. It certainly shows how far she had come from Henry James. Yet the latter, who always recognized the first rate, even when its form was at variance with his theories, might have approved of *My Ántonia*. He shared, after all, its author's passionate admiration for Stevenson, whose loose, easily flowing nostalgic narratives are far closer to the Nebraska novels than *The Golden Bowl* or *The Wings of the Dove*.

One may speculate that Willa Cather wrote *My Ántonia* very much as Jim Burden says *he* wrote it and that its shape, such as it is, is dictated by actual reminiscence. She freely admitted that Ántonia was closely modeled on Anna Pavelka, who had occupied in her childhood the same focal position that Ántonia had occupied in Burden's. Miss Cather was never much interested in what was or what was not a "novel." Fact, fancy, reminiscence, invention, what difference did it make? The mood, the unity, the finished product was all.

Elizabeth Sergeant describes a visit of Willa Cather to her apartment while she was still in the throes of putting her novel together:

"She then suddenly leaned over — and this is something I remembered clearly when *My Ántonia* came into my hands, at last, in 1918 — and set an old Sicilian apothecary jar of mine, filled with orange-brown flowers of scented stock, in the middle of a bare, round, antique table. 'I want my new heroine to be like this — like a rare object in the middle of a table, which one may examine from all sides.' "

Yet certainly Ántonia is not seen from all sides. One has only the dimmest conception of her relation with her seducer, and there is a great deal about her life as a hired girl that remains in the shadows. What is seen from all sides, being turned slowly for the reader like a statue on a revolving platform, is Jim Burden's (Willa Cather's) memory of Ántonia, and this becomes a thing complete in itself, so we are not disturbed by the missing pieces in Ántonia. It is not, therefore, so much a book about Ántonia as a book about someone's memory of Ántonia, in short, a book about nostalgia.

The relevance of all the details, including the terrible story of the wolves, is simply their relevance to Miss Cather. She selected, probably by a purely subjective test, the scenes and incidents that came to mind most vividly about her Nebraska childhood. The result, by whatever design, is triumphant. The finished work is bathed in the serene, golden mood of recaptured time. The "precious, the incommunicable past" *has* been communicated. It has become almost synonymous with the flat, endless Nebraska plains and rough, shaggy, tall red grass over which, as it seemed to the young Jim Burden, one could walk to the very edge of the earth. "The light air about me told me that the world ended here: only the ground and sun and sky were left, and if one went a little farther there would be only sun and sky, and one would float off into them, like the tawny hawks which sailed over our heads making slow shadows on the grass."

Ántonia, with her love, her patience, her philosophic acceptance of betrayal, her honesty and simplicity, contains the soul of the land and its pioneer farmers. "She had only to stand in the orchard, to put her hand on a little crab tree and look up at the apples, to make you feel the goodness of planting and tending and harvesting at last. . . . She was a rich mine of life, like the founders of early races." She is more than a figure remembered; she is the very process of remembering. Willa Cather was to equal this accomplishment in the future; she was never to surpass it.

Miss Cather always felt that she had published *The Troll Garden* prematurely, and in 1920 she brought out *Youth and the Bright Medusa* which contained the best of the earlier volume with some more recent stories. There are two interrelated themes in the collection: the impact of art upon westerners, poor in purse but still poorer in culture, and a comparison of the dedicated to the merely popular artist. "Coming, Aphrodite!" — dealing with the latter theme — records the brief summer love affair between Don Hedger, a truculently independent painter, and Eden Bower, a beautiful but spiritually commonplace opera singer whose nude calisthenics he has been watching through a knothole in their boardinghouse. In the end, Eden, now a great star, visits an art gallery to check on her former lover and discovers to her relief that his talent has been recognized. "One doesn't like to have been an utter fool, even at twenty."

"The Diamond Mine" and "Paul's Case" are the two best stories in the book. The first is Willa Cather's single successful description of an opera star in her days of stardom. Cressida Garnet is eaten alive by greedy husbands and greedy relatives and finds only a brief happiness with a fiery Bohemian composer, who loses his fire with domestication and succumbs to the *gâteaux* and charms of Cressida's cook. Only death on the *Titanic* saves Cressida from bankruptcy. "Paul's Case," justly Willa Cather's most widely anthologized short story, is an extraordinary capture of the fantasy mood of a young man in a small town who embezzles money from his employer to enjoy the luxury of a few days in a deluxe Manhattan hotel.

The other four stories, unfortunately, are spoiled by the shrillness of the author's anger against a world that fails to appreciate artists. "A Wagner Matinée" shows what seems a too violent reaction of an old music-starved Nebraskan woman to a concert. "The Sculptor's Funeral" is a rather lachrymose elegy for an artist who cannot vend his wares. "A Gold Slipper" and "Scandal," both dealing with the great singer Kitty Ayrshire, continue to explore the artist's troubles with a Philistine world after success has been achieved. But Kitty has too much of everything to be believable: too much beauty and wit and philosophy, too much talent and grace and charm. Willa Cather failed to appreciate the dangers of star worship; she did not see that the opera fan who likes to imagine herself as Geraldine Farrar or Olive Fremstad is very much the same as the shop girl who pictures herself as Marlene Dietrich or Elizabeth Taylor. When Kitty speaks of men seeing in women only "some cheap conception of prettiness you got from a coloured supplement when you were adolescents," one wonders where Willa Cather got hers of Kitty. There was always a *Movie Mirror* side to her enthrallment with concert and operatic success.

World War I inspired its sideline observers with a drum-beating hysteria and a high scorn of the enemy that was quite unlike anything produced by its successor. This was particularly true among artists who had no personal stake in the fighting. Amy Lowell read aloud her poem "Bombardment" for Belgian War Relief with a man concealed behind the platform to strike a drum at each "boom," and Edith Wharton lost her sense of what mothers feel to the point of writing an American friend: "You must be having thrilling times with both the boys in the war already." Willa Cather, a slow starter, escaped some of this mood, largely because her real concern with the war followed it and was toned down by postwar disillusionment. But much of the hysteria nonetheless seeped into her worst novel and, ironically, her single Pulitzer Prize winner, *One of Ours* (1922).

Like so many war books, it is really two novels: a before and an after. The "after" contains a number of fighting scenes in France which are certainly not good when contrasted with those of Erich Maria Remarque or Norman Mailer, but which are not bad if considered as exercises by a nonparticipant who has done her research conscientiously. It is difficult to regard them in any light other than as a tour de force by the author of *My Ántonia*. Such merit as they do possess is clouded over by the writer's attitude of moral superiority, as, for example, when her hero finds on the corpse of an aristocratic German officer a miniature, not of the officer's best girl, but of his best boy. Typical, no doubt, of the decadent Kaiser's court!

The boyhood and youth of Claude Wheeler on a Nebraska farm is, as might be expected, handled more competently, but the section shares some of Claude's dullness. He seems oddly incapable of any effective action. He knows that he wants to be educated and that his family can easily afford it, yet when his unimaginative but not unsympathetic father suggests that he give up college to help with the farm, he does so with death in his heart but without a word of protest. Similarly, he perversely insists on courting Enid Royce, despite every warning (including her own) that she is a frigid religious fanatic, and at last overcomes her well-grounded aversion to marriage. One has seen such courtships in everyday life and the wretched unions that follow them, but Willa Cather never probes into the real motivations. Why? Why must she make Claude so sluggish, inert, dead? Simply because he has to be awakened and redeemed by Europe and battle.

We see the headlines of the Archduke's assassination through Nebraskan eyes and watch Claude and his mother (who has not previously shown any interest in anything) poring over maps at night to chart the German advance on the kitchen table. And then he signs up (his wife has already gone to China as a missionary), and we are subjected to the war with all its jingle and jangle, and nonsense about French culture as silly as Edith Wharton ever wrote at her most bellicose. In a few brief leaves, under the spell of a soldier musician who knows all about art and beauty, Claude discovers that life, after all, may be worth living and that the real death was in that airless farmhouse at home. When he is killed in the end, a hero, and America reverts to a sluggish peace and the error of her old ways, Miss Cather suggests somberly that it may be just as well. Had he survived, he would probably have committed suicide, like the others: "One by one the heroes of that war, the men of dazzling soldiership, leave prematurely the world they have come back to. Airmen whose deeds were tales of wonder, officers whose names made the blood of youth beat faster, survivors of incredible dangers,— one by one they quietly die by their own hand."

Willa Cather once said that in 1922 the world had broken in two and that she belonged to the earlier half, but this statement was simply the culmination of a habit of thinking that had begun before the war. In a review of the play *Potash and Perlmutter* in *McClure's* early in 1914, she inveighed against the deterioration of city life in phrases that might have been written by Sinclair Lewis, whom she was later greatly to admire. "This city roars and rumbles and hoots and jangles because Potash and Perlmutter are on their way to something." The ugly clothes that New Yorkers had to buy, the garish, jerrybuilt monster apartment houses in which they had to live, were dictated by the bad taste of Potash and Perlmutter. This preoccupation with the cheapness and tawdriness of the twentieth century was to eat even more deeply into Willa Cather's heart than it ate into Edith Wharton's or Ellen Glasgow's. Luckily, however, for the artist in her, she had something with which to balance it. She had her vision of the past.

It had not existed, the past, in the endless prairies of Nebraska or in its hot little towns. It had existed in Virginia, but she had left Virginia as a child. For the stocky, plain, hardworking girl, surrounded by the intellectually unsympathetic, beauty had to be torn out of books. Later, there were glimpses of it in the theater and opera and trips to Europe, but they failed to give her what she really needed: a bridge from a European past to an American present, or better yet, a bridge from an American past to an American present. This latter past she had not discovered until 1912 on her trip to the Southwest, when it had burst upon her with profound effect. As there were no historical links between the Pueblo Indians and twentieth-century Americans, any bridge had to be a mystical one, and her attempt to create it was to give a unique quality to her later work and to save her from degenerating into a shrill and ineffective female version of H. L. Mencken.

In 1922, her year of division, she was confirmed into the Episcopalian Church. The split between the woman and the artist was from now on to be increasingly distinct, one hostile to the disarray of the times, more and more conservative, even reactionary, the other immersed in the very special task of working a rich spiritual pattern out of the bits and pieces of the past.

A Lost Lady (1923) is as charming a tale as *One of Ours* is cumbersome and as well organized as its predecessor is loose and rambling. It is the simple story of a lovely lady who falls from grace when her husband's strength ceases to protect her. As one half of a happy couple she is perfection itself; alone, she is lost. Certainly, in terms of charm, she is the most attractive of Willa Cather's heroines. George Jean Nathan said: "All of Willa Cather's characters smell of Ivory soap, even the 'bad' women, and that's something I don't believe. Sin doesn't smell like soap, it smells like perfume — cheap perfume, perhaps, but perfume." But Marian Forrester suggests the most expensive Chanel.

We see her mostly (but not entirely) through the eyes of young Niel Herbert, nephew and assistant of the local lawyer in Sweet Water of the western prairies. She is a beautiful, graceful creature, kind to everybody and of an exquisite tact and friendliness, married to the local tycoon, Captain Forrester, some twenty-five years her senior, who has won her gratitude and her hand by rescuing her from an accident in the wilderness. He is represented as being of the race of titans who made the old West, "who put plains and mountains under iron harness." Carving a turkey for company he recalls the splendid if patronizing good manners of the Duc de Guermantes in *The Guermantes Way*. The Forresters are perfectly happy, despite their differences in age and temperament, until the Captain loses both his health and his money. Marian tends him faithfully, but as his physical strength deteriorates, so does her moral fortitude. She has an affair with the flashy Frank Ellinger, and, after the Captain's death, allows herself to be shabby and talked about, giving supper parties for young men and becoming the mistress of Ivy Peters, a revolting fellow, a kind of Uriah Heep whom we have first seen slitting the eyes of a live woodpecker in the most horrible scene, with the possible exception of the wolf pack in *My Ántonia*, in all Miss Cather's fiction.

Willa Cather's simple moral is that Marian is symptomatic of the post-pioneer generation: she has style but no guts. Niel Herbert's heart aches as he watches her descend the social scale, though the reader, if not he, is delighted in the end by the last-minute reversal in her fortunes when she captures and marries a rich old Argentinian. What Niel most holds against her is that she was not willing "to immolate herself, like the widows of all these great men, and die with the pioneer period to which she belonged; that she preferred life on any terms." But she makes a charming memory.

After *My Ántonia* Miss Cather decided to change publishers. Although she always remained a good friend of Ferris Greenslet, she did not feel that the other editors of Houghton Mifflin appreciated her work, nor was she satisfied with the format of her novels or the promotion accorded them. When she first called on Alfred Knopf she found a publisher after her own heart. On his desk were samples of blue paper which he had procured from the Metropolitan Museum of Art "to find exactly the right shade among the Chinese blues" for a volume of Chinese poetry that he was bringing out. The relationship formed between him and Miss Cather was a most satisfactory one, lasting until her death, and it earned them both a great deal of money.

There are those, largely, one suspects, of academic circles, who consider *The Professor's House* (1925) Willa Cather's most interesting novel. It is, indeed, a mine for symbol seekers. Godfrey St. Peter, professor of history at a small college on Lake Michigan, has at last gained a bit of money and reputation with his eight-volume history about Spanish explorers in America and has built a new house, but finds himself sentimentally unable to abandon the old, where he did his lifework. He and his family, consisting of his wife, Lillian, two daughters, Rosamond and Kathleen, and their husbands, are all shadowed by the memory of Tom Outland, a brilliant student at the university who was killed in the war. Rosamond had been engaged to him and received under his will a patent which has made her and her greasy husband rich and snobbish. Kathleen had also been in love with Outland, and her husband had been his best friend, and they are soured by envy of Rosamond's wealth. Their mother, and to some extent St. Peter himself, are represented as having been vaguely corrupted by the indirect benefits of Rosamond's money. Also Professor Crane, an old friend who shared in the development but not the profits of Outland's patent, consumed by bitterness, has been reduced to the meanness of a futile lawsuit against Rosamond and her husband.

As in *One of Ours* the note is struck that Tom Outland, dead in the war, is better off than any of them. St. Peter, left alone while his wife travels with Rosamond and her husband in Europe, thinks back on a story that Tom Outland once told him of how he and a friend, Blake, climbed a mesa in the Southwest to find the ruins of an unknown, archaic Indian village. The story is here inserted in the book, and we learn how Outland goes to Washington to interest the Smithsonian in his find. While he is wrangling with bureaucrats there, Blake, an ignorant cowpuncher, innocently sells the pottery and other artifacts to a German archaeologist who has instantly grasped their true value. Outland, furious at what he considers a betrayal of the trust imposed by their discovery, breaks with Blake who goes off, never to be seen again, leaving his friend to the tardy recognition that he will have somehow to pay for having so maltreated him.

Willa Cather later wrote that she meant Outland's story to have the effect of a window in a Dutch painting of an interior: it was to bring in the sun and out-of-doors, in fact all the movement of a busy harbor, to a stuffy, ordered, middle-class living room, to the St. Peters' new living room itself. One may be struck by this idea, and still doubt that she brought it off. Outland's story is a very fine piece of writing, but it is completely independent in itself. In reading it, one forgets the professor's house and afterwards returns a bit reluctantly to the St. Peters and their doings. A novel is not like a painting where one can see two things at once — at least not as Miss Cather writes it.

After his recollections Professor St. Peter is almost asphyxiated by the stove in his old study. The circumstances suggest a passivity amounting to suicidal impulse. Rescued, he becomes reconciled to living out the balance of his life. Willa Cather seems to be saying that even though there are things in life more beautiful than men and women and domestic burdens and the daily grind, i.e. the discovery of the mesa village, the writing of *Spanish Adventurers in North America*, one must not pursue them, as has Outland, at the cost of a friend, or, as has St. Peter, at the cost of a family. But why all the false leads? What about Kathleen and Outland? Were they really in love? What happened to Professor Crane's lawsuit? Why is it really necessary for St. Peter to live on for children who no longer need him and a wife who no longer really cares? Miss Cather's theory of not violating her original conception, of not fitting it into an artificial plot, seems for once to have produced a notebook rather than a finished novel.

The ever obliging Alfred Knopf, always willing to bring out even the slenderest volumes of Willa Cather's prose — an author's dream of an editor — outdid himself in 1926 when he published a short story handsomely bound between hard covers. Yet *My Mortal Enemy* was worth it. It is one of the finest pieces Miss Cather ever wrote and gains by being presented alone. Myra Driscoll is the study of a strong, stubborn, bitter woman, an aging Cordelia who now passionately regrets that she has given up a kingdom for the momentary satisfaction of frustrating an old man's whim. For she has defied a relentless great-uncle and lost a fortune to marry Oswald Henshawe, a decent if sentimental man whose primary claim to Myra's affection was the aversion that he inspired in her rich relative. Through the sympathetic eye of an old friend we see Myra grow more and more bitter as her circumstances deteriorate until at last she lies slowly dying in a cheap boardinghouse, lovingly tended by the faithful husband whom she now loathes as her "mortal enemy" and whose financial ruin she has helped to accomplish by openly despising his business friends.

It is astonishing how much pity Willa Cather engenders for this character. For all her selfishness and self-indulgence Myra has a curious magnificence. In her final poverty she has yet a cache of gold coins to buy masses for the soul of the great actress Helena Modjeska (her Fremstad), who represents all the beauty of the world out of which Myra has cheated herself. That she has brought it all on herself more by her meanness than by her marriage, that she is evidently a woman who would have been unhappy under any circumstances, simply adds to her pathos. A reader might become a bit weary of Myra in a full-length novel or fail to understand her in a shorter story; the medium chosen is exactly right for the subject and its treatment.

Willa Cather had now discovered that in using the past she did not have to limit herself to the past of her own or even of her parents' recollection. Indeed, the further back she went, the closer she seemed to approach the essence of that pioneer spirit from which she felt that the twentieth century was a tragic falling away. It is certainly healthier for a novelist to admire the past than to deplore the present. Edith Wharton was on the same right track when she wrote *The Age of Innocence,* as was Ellen Glasgow in the early chapters of *Vein of Iron,* but the right track, alas, was the exception and not, as with Willa Cather, the rule, in their later work. Miss Cather allowed the woman but never the writer to become a crank.

Death Comes for the Archbishop (1927) was her most popular and is, in some ways, her most excellent novel. The loose, easy plot is shaped by the biographies of two nineteenth-century French missionary priests, called in the novel Jean Marie Latour and Joseph Vaillant, who almost single-handedly took over and reconstructed the Roman Catholic church in the new southwestern territory which is now New Mexico and Arizona. As these priests, under other names, actually lived, the episodic character of the narrative has a certain justification in fact. But the real common denominator is the glory of the southwest landscape described in a lyric prose that is the summit of the author's achievement.

There is nothing more vivid in American fiction than this series of brilliant pictures of an arid, glowing country: the cruciform tree amid the endless conical red sandhills of the desert that leads the parched Father Latour to a stream; the hill of golden colored stone on a ridge over the Rio Grande Valley that becomes the quarry for his great cathedral in Santa Fé; the flat white outline — a square made up of squares — that was the pueblo, or rock, of Ácoma where the natives retreated for centuries to escape from raiding Navajos and where an early misguided missionary made them, like Egyptian slaves, build a gaunt, grim, gray fortress of a church. Against such backgrounds Willa Cather recounts her wonderful tales of local characters: the schismatic Padre Martínez who lives surrounded by his offspring like a Renaissance pope, the vain Doña Isabella who risks losing a fortune rather than tell her true age in a lawsuit, the fiend who slaughters travelers seeking a night's lodging in the desert wilderness. The whole compilation is suffused with a feeling of high Christian serenity of purpose as peaceful as the twilight view of Rome from the cardinal's terrace in the great prologue where the troublesome new world is seen through the undazzled eyes of the old, where cactus deserts and Indians seem not quite real amid the civilized clink of silver and glass.

There are moments, here and there, when the reader feels almost as far away from the Southwest as those distant Roman diners, when the novel seems to take on some of the quality of a children's story, too calm, too seraphic, too bathed in nostalgia for a braver, simpler time. In a letter to the editor of the *Commonweal* Willa Cather wrote that she had tried for the effect of Puvis de Chavannes' frescoes of the life of Saint Genevieve, "something without accent, with none of the artificial elements of composition." All human experiences, she maintained, great and trivial, when measured against "one supreme spiritual experience" should be of about the same importance. But Miss Cather did better than Puvis de Chavannes whose figures are stilted and whose colors are pale. A truer comparison would be to Poussin. Violence, rape, and murder may occur in Poussin's paintings and even be faithfully detailed, but the over-all effect is nonetheless one of classic stillness and control. He and Willa Catha possessed the artistic detachment needed for this particular aesthetic effect. Their passion expressed itself riotously only in color.

The paradox in Willa Cather's theory of fiction, the novel démeublé, or stripped of all unnecessary descriptions and stratagems, the novel that must almost flow by some process of artistic free association from a mind that has fully assimilated the characters and scenes to be portrayed, is that she herself did not abide by it. Although her completed novels may be somewhat shapeless, they are filled with little gems of short stories, insets, that might have been conceived and plotted by Guy de Maupassant himself. Critics have leaned over backwards to relate these to the novels in which they appear, and critics who are not themselves novelists are apt to make wide allowances for seeming irrelevancies in this respect. E. K. Brown, for example, finds the long Tom Outland story of the discovery of the mesa in *The Professor's House* a "perfect placing," though even he is less sure about the wolf-pack tale in *My Ántonia*. Yet it is difficult not to suspect that the latter is dragged in purely because Miss Cather loved it and would not leave it out, and that the former, although essential to the plot of the novel — the whole point in fact — is awkwardly introduced.

The historical novel not only served to eliminate Willa Cather's grudges against modern life; it provided the skeleton on which the most disparate and unconnected matters could be hung. *Death Comes for the Archbishop* is like a gallery of brilliantly lit dioramas in a historical museum illustrating life in the American Southwest a century ago. Everything falls into place because the reader accepts the era and the locale as in themselves creating a frame and hence a form. It is the same in *Shadows on the Rock* (1931), a series of quiet scenes in and about the youth of Cécile Auclair, the daughter of Euclide Auclair, who is apothecary to the Count de Frontenac, governor of the small French colony of Quebec at the end of the seventeenth century.

Even less happens by way of plot than in *Death Comes for the Archbishop* and even more by way of "insets." Cécile, at twelve, keeps house for her father, a widower and an intellectual whose advanced medical ideas are tolerated by the prejudiced community in which he lives only because of the Count's patronage. She befriends a small sad boy whose mother is the town prostitute; she is taken for a rustic visit to the Île d'Orléans by Pierre Charron, a younger friend of her father's and a fur trader (we learn in the epilogue that she marries him), and she sees the ships come in after the "long winter" with the expected recall of the Count and, accordingly, of her father. But, as it turns out, there is no recall; Frontenac dies, knowing that he has been forgotten, and the Auclairs resign themselves to living permanently in the new world. For Cécile, however, there is more than resignation. There is hope and happiness. She and Pierre have come over young enough to transfer their roots, and Canada has become their home.

That is all, rather less than in *Death Comes for the Archbishop*. Yet the fact that less time elapses and less geography is covered (to give a nod in the direction of the classic unities) gives the story its greater concentration of mood. It perfectly evokes the dull, quiet, rigorous life of that precarious little colony perched on a high rock like the seabirds who come to nest on the naked islands of the Gulf of St. Lawrence. Why are these people there? Why do they stay? They are not sure themselves. The older ones, like the Count and the apothecary, hanker for France; they have courage and enterprise and determination but no deep and abiding love for that great gray crag that rises up between a cruel sea and a relentless forest. The Count's ultimate acceptance of death in this exile makes an affecting chapter, as does his account of his final interview with Louis XIV, who cannot distract his attention from feeding the carp at Fontainebleau long enough to pay any real heed to the soldier who has spent his life on the frontier of his empire. Yet there is little bitterness in Frontenac; he is like all the older settlers who long for France and accept the fact that France is bound to forget them.

The insets have more coherence to the novel's scheme than those of *Death Comes for the Archbishop*, for they illustrate religious themes and intensify the Catholic atmosphere in which Miss Cather chooses to see the little colony bathed. They deal largely with the sufferings of the deeply devout: the appalling self-entombment of Jeanne Le Ber, the recluse, which brings her neither repose nor happiness after twenty years; the agonized repentance of Blinker, who had been apprenticed in France in the hideous trade of torture and fears himself damned; the terrible doubts of the missionary Chabanel, who cannot forgive himself for his feelings of disgust and revulsion at his foul-smelling Indian converts. Yet none of their agitations can disturb the underlying serenity of the Canadian scene. Once again the total effect is of a Poussin.

The most important aspect of these two historical novels is the new light that they shed on the ancient "international problem," so dear to the hearts of Henry James and his disciples. The Jacobites were apt to see the problem in terms of the effect of a wicked old Europe, charming, cultivated, but deeply corrupt, on a young, idealistic visitor from over the seas, undereducated, raw, but pure. There was always a dash of soap opera in this conception, of a mustachioed count and a blonde heroine, and this intrusion of so low an element comes not from any artistic deficiency in Jacobites but in a bit of alloy, a bit of basic superficiality in the theme itself. Was the international problem really a "problem" as so conceived, any more than overcharging hotels or gouging restaurants or other annoyances that await the tourist? Miss Cather, who had traveled extensively in Europe, saw that the vital aspect of the "problem" was the impact of the new world on the old *in* the new world.

She had always been concerned with it, from her earliest days in Red Cloud when she had observed the Bohemians on their farms and noted that although the old might learn to cope with Nebraska, only the young could ever really learn to like it. The suicide of Mr. Shimerda, the emigrant who has failed, appears as a theme in one of her earliest college stories. Later she came to relate the problem to art, and for a long time she saw rural America as a benighted area cut off from the life-giving springs of European culture. Claude Wheeler in *One of Ours* may die in the trenches, but his glimpse of French culture is supposed to be worth it. This is silly enough, but it is silly because it represents the one instance where Willa Cather approached the international problem conventionally. It is far better when she brings European art to America and considers the effect of Wagner on Thea Kronborg. *That* was the vital thing, and she studied it consciously, taking a particular interest in opera singers who had been born or raised in America: Lillian Nordica, Geraldine Farrar, Olive Fremstad. To hear the Walkyries over the plains of the West was more exciting than to see an American lad "reeling and moaning" (to use James' own words) through the beautiful streets of Rome.

If Willa Cather started with the impact of America on poor immigrants and went on to explore the impact of European culture on America, she ended, most significantly, with the impact of America on educated European pioneers. It is her vision of Father Latour's vision of the Southwest and of Pierre Chardon's vision of Canada that is her highest achievement. Neither Latour nor Pierre ever want to go back; they have seen a beauty as fine as anything that elicited the gasps of the young Henry James. In *Death Comes for the Archbishop* there is quite as deep a sense of the past as in *The Ambassadors*. The mesas are as old as anything in Paris, and eternity broods over the desert. Henry Adams was one of the few American writers of his time to find as much in America and in the Pacific to stimulate his imagination as in Europe. It is a pity that he did not survive to comment on Miss Cather's historical novels.

Obscure Destinies (1932), a book of stories, is a return to the Nebraska of Willa Cather's childhood and contains writing as fine as any to be found even in *My Ántonia*. "Neighbour Rosicky" is the tale of an old Bohemian of Mr. Shimerda's generation who does his touching best to make farm life palatable to a village-bred daughter-in-law; he is as fitting a symbol of the land as Ántonia or Alexandra Bergson. "Old Mrs. Harris" is modeled on Miss Cather's own grandmother, reduced to the status of a household servant by her selfish daughter. The poor old woman's one ambition in servitude is to spare her wretched child from the just criticisms of the neighbors. Both stories could easily tumble into the trough of sentimentality, but they do not; that is Willa Cather's triumph, as it is Victor Hugo's and Zola's.

Willa Cather, with the exception of *One of Ours*, maintained an extraordinarily high level in her fiction, but *Lucy Gayheart* (1935) suggests an attenuation of powers. It is a rather faded and sentimental version of *The Song of the Lark*. The craft is all there, and the style, but the subject matter is not worthy of them. Lucy, the heroine, has charm and a touching desire to live and be happy, but that is all. She is no Thea Kronborg; her interest in music is quite subordinated to her interest in men, and the middle-aged singer Clement Sebastian with whom she falls in love is at best a shadowy character. Harry Gordon, the rich young banker from Lucy's hometown who takes her to the opera and takes her for granted, whistling Wagner off tune and calling her "Lucy mio," is far more vivid. Piqued by his fatuous assumption that she will be only too honored to become his bride, Lucy tells him that she is Sebastian's mistress, a misrepresentation that leads directly to what little tragedy there is in the book. Harry, angry and humiliated, marries a plain, unloving woman, and, passing Lucy on foot in his sleigh one cold winter day, he ungallantly refuses her a lift. Lucy is drowned, skating home over the thin ice of the river, and Harry is condemned to a long life of sterile remorse. It is a sad little tale of misunderstandings and youthful heartache, charmingly done, rather like a gentle and sensitive "art" film produced for the *cognoscenti* on a low budget.

The last of the novels, *Sapphira and the Slave Girl* (1940), is in parts equal to the best of what went before. It is set in the Virginia of Willa Cather's childhood but of a period twenty years before her birth, about which she could have known only by family tradition and hearsay. Angus Wilson once pointed out in a lecture that an astonishing number of the greatest English novels are placed in the era immediately preceding their authors' births. It may come from a tendency in artists to think of their childhood as occurring in the evening of a romantic era which must have had its apex before they were born. But, of course, the antebellum South has become in our century a symbol of romance to everyone.

Miss Cather, however, by limiting herself in this novel to the geography of her childhood, cut herself off from the cavaliers and the most ebullient part of the legend. She was intent on making the country of her birth the frame for an intimate study of the peculiar institution. Sapphira Dodderidge, of Virginia's best, to the astonishment of her friends and family, elects to marry a miller and move with her dozen slaves to the backwoods where no one else has any, and to become a large, complacent frog in a very small puddle. Imperious, just (when not blinded by jealousy), clear-minded, orderly, shrewd, and invalided with dropsy, she accepts the misfortunes that come to herself and to others with equal stoicism. But above all she is the mistress, the slave owner; that is the cancer that destroys her soul and misshapes her, as it misshapes her slaves, making them the funny, loyal, antic darky dolls of legend, instead of men and women. And this whole grisly performance owes half of its grisliness to the fact that it is acted out before the disapproving eyes of a non-slaveholding community, including Sapphira's own husband and daughter. Sapphira and her slaves assume that they are life as life should be, but to the onlookers they are a macabre vaudeville. How her daughter Rachel shudders at the bland, sarcastic tone that her mother uses to the erring Negro! It is the horror of her childhood.

Vaudeville turns into something far uglier when Sapphira suspects (unjustly, as it turns out) that her husband covets the slave girl Nancy. She begins to persecute the poor bewildered girl, a former favorite of hers, in a dozen minor ways, but when her husband, whose consent is legally necessary, refuses to sell Nancy, the real trouble begins. Sapphira, determined now to ruin the girl, invites a worthless nephew of her husband, a notorious libertine, to make a long visit and assigns Nancy to do his room. She even goes so far as to send her on errands in parts of the countryside where he is riding alone. In judging the inhumanity of this — and we see it through Nancy's terror-stricken eyes — we should remember H. G. Wells's caveat about judging the Roman emperors: how do we know how *we* would behave with absolute power over our fellow humans? Sapphira, who considers herself a good and conscientious woman and a just mistress, never suffers a single qualm of conscience, and when her daughter Rachel finally saves the miserable Nancy by the dangerous expedient of sending her North on the underground railway, her mother solemnly breaks relations with her. Yet she resumes them when Rachel's little daughter dies. Sapphira is not a fiend.

Not a fiend, perhaps, yet for her own personal convenience she has married Nancy's mother, Till, to a "capon man." But that was the system, a system that made it possible for a brave, strongminded, cultivated woman, without a trace of shame, to turn a helpless girl over to the mercy of a brute. Why not? Would the girl really mind it as a white girl would? Sapphira is the most memorable of Willa Cather's characters — excepting Ántonia — regal enough just to escape the ridiculous as she is borne about in a chair by her loving darkies, a backwoods Queen Bess, always a pageant to herself and her slaves. No matter if the others laughed. What sort of trash were they, anyway? The real world was back in Winchester where Sapphira went once a year to visit her married sister, leaving her husband and daughter behind.

After *Sapphira* Willa Cather wrote only a few inferior, rather tired tales, published posthumously in *The Old Beauty and Others* (1948) and some short nonfiction pieces. In 1942 she had a gallbladder operation from which she never fully recovered. She lived on, in the Park Avenue apartment that she had rented after the demolition of No. 5 Bank Street, enjoying her friends and music and occasional shortened walks in Central Park, until 1947. Mildred R. Bennett says of her in *The World of Willa Cather*: "She contended that she had only a certain number of stories to write, a certain amount of cremated youth, and when she had done these, she would be written out. Others might have their professions and talents: her 'only assets' were her stories. Perhaps in this lies an explanation for her withdrawal. As she burned herself away in her writing, she had less and less to give; and she did not have that saving sense of humor which has from the beginning of time enabled others to laugh at themselves. Her religion of Art she took very seriously."

On her tombstone in Jaffrey, New Hampshire, the village where she wrote *My Ántonia*, is this quotation from the novel: "That is happiness; to be dissolved into something complete and great."

5

ELIZABETH MADOX ROBERTS

IF Emily Brontë had survived the publication of *Wuthering Heights* to write a series of obscure and ponderous allegorical novels, would her reputation be as splendid as it is today? One may doubt it. There is something about the image of a life seemingly offered up on the altar of literature as the price of one perfect book that becomes part of the atmosphere in which the book is read. If Elizabeth Madox Roberts had disappeared from the literary scene after the publication of her first novel, *The Time of Man*, in 1926, she might stand today in the company of Willa Cather and Ellen Glasgow. For as a lyrical evocation of the farmer's relation to the soil it is quite the equal of *My Ántonia* and *Barren Ground*.

Her life was dogged by poverty and ill health, and she was born amid bitter memories. Her father, Simpson Roberts, at fourteen saw his own father shot in cold blood for refusing to join the National Guard and at sixteen joined the Confederate Army. He and his wife, both of pioneer stock, struggled through a Kentucky reconstruction and survived with a small grocery on the first floor of their house in Springfield and with Mr. Roberts' ultimate appointment as engineer and surveyor of the county. The county was in the fertile and hilly farm region that his daughter was to describe so vividly.

She was born in 1881, the first of eight children, and had to start early to help with the household work. She did well at school and yearned to go to college; she did enroll at the State College of Kentucky but her uncertain health and the family's lack of means kept her from completing the course. A shy, frail, introverted, rather lovely girl, she lived with her family and opened a small private school for children at a tuition of three dollars per month. She taught from a rocking chair and sometimes fainted in the classroom. Later, when her health improved, she taught in the public schools and published some poetry. In 1917, when she was thirty-six, there was at last enough money to enable her to realize her dream and enroll as a freshman in the University of Chicago. Harry M. Campbell and Ruel E. Foster, authors of the deeply perceptive if perhaps overlaudatory *Elizabeth Madox Roberts, American Novelist*, describe her at this period: "She had an original, quiet intelligence with an inward poetic cast. Her sensibility was a complex one. There was in the world of her mind a long wind blowing out of the past, out of Virginia and Maryland and Harrodsburg, Kentucky, from the days of Daniel Boone and James Harrod: a wind bringing old phrases, old talk, and the personalities of long-dead ancestry to life."

She made many good friends, despite her age difference, in what turned out to be an exceedingly talented class; she specialized in English literature and the philosophic idealism of Bishop Berkeley, and she was elected to Phi Beta Kappa. Her classmate Glenway Wescott recalls her as "the young southern woman, alone absolutely original, unimpressed by the setting of evils and plagiaries, meek and insinuatingly affirmative, untouched by but kindly toward all our half-grown baseness." She was drawn to Catholicism, an attraction that was to endure for life, but she never became a convert.

After college Miss Roberts returned to her family in Springfield. At the age of forty-one, in the fall of 1922, her education was at last completed, and she devoted her mornings to the composition of *The Time of Man*. Three years later, with considerable interludes for writing poetry, it was completed, accepted by the Viking Press, and chosen by the Book-of-the-Month Club. It had an immediate critical and popular success, and Miss Roberts found herself at once relieved of obscurity and financial need. She could never induce her parents to abandon their old home, so she added a large brick wing containing a study and library. There, amid high shelves of books, she was to spend the bulk of her days, although in the later years her health drove her to Florida in the winter.

Miss Roberts' notes for *The Time of Man* show that she conceived it as an Odyssey, with her heroine as the eternal wanderer. The six parts into which she divided the book do not correspond to any chapter division in the text, but rather to the symphonic movements of her idea of the story:

I. A Genesis. She comes into the land. But the land rejects her. She remembers Eden (Tessie).
II. She grows into the land, takes soil or root. Life tries her, lapses into lovelessness . . .
III. Expands with all the land.
IV. The first blooming.
V. Withdrawal — and sinking back into the earth.
VI. Flowering out of stone.

Ellen Chesser, the sole surviving child of itinerant farmers, Henry and Nellie, is constantly on the move with her parents through the rural areas of Kentucky. She yearns for permanent things, for houses that are more than shacks, with drawers to put things in, and friends who are more than passing acquaintances. This yearning centers in Tessie, a loquacious semi-gypsy given to flights of imagination, from whom Ellen is separated and whom she vainly seeks, running away from the farm on which her father settles for a time. After this single rebellion, her one practical attempt to recapture Eden, she settles down, "growing into the land," and Jonas Prather seems to offer marriage and "blooming." But after he has confided in her the secret of his affair with a prostitute and of the child that he believes to be his own, he identifies her with the guilt of which he has made her the repository and deserts her for another. Ellen rejects the temptation of suicide, the example of which is offered by Mrs. MacMurtrie, of the local gentry, who hangs herself when her husband goes off with her cousin, and finds the blooming that Jonas Prather had seemed to offer with Jasper Kent, a strong, violent man and an itinerant farmer like her father.

She and Jasper have several children, and she seems at last in tune with the natural things that surround her. But the withdrawal, the "sinking back into earth," occurs suddenly and horribly when Jasper, an adulterer himself, wildly and irrationally accuses her of infidelity and repudiates the child she is carrying. Only when the child is born, a shrunken, sickly bit of a thing, does he repent, but it is too late. The child, suffering from its mother's shock, lives three miserable years and dies. And then Jasper is beaten up by night riders who mistakenly believe him to be a barn burner, and he insists on packing up and moving on. The "flowering out of stone" occurs when Ellen, realizing that her destiny is irretrievably linked with his, refuses to be left behind, and the Kents move away together in their old wagon with all their few poor goods, asking no directions on the road, taking their own turnings.

To tell this story Miss Roberts limits her points of view to Ellen Chesser's and her own, but she does not pretend to limit herself to Ellen Chesser's simple vocabulary. Ellen, after all, is uneducated. Miss Roberts uses her lyrical prose to convey to the reader the state of being Ellen, which is a far more complicated thing than Ellen could possibly articulate. Ellen loves the countryside and all its creatures, even the pigs that must be slaughtered; she is vitally aware of sound and color, of sun and seasons, of affection and distrust. Her extreme sensitivity is conveyed in a prose-poetry that is at times full of sharp, precise imagery and at times dreamlike in its flowing smoothness.

Ellen Glasgow doubted that rural people talked like the characters in *The Time of Man*. Perhaps they do not. Miss Roberts was searching in her dialogue for a rhythm that would convey the inner as well as the outer man and that would give a sense of the people as a unit and a fraction of the geography. It was part of what she called the "poetic realism" that she tried to achieve in all her prose. "Somewhere there is a connection between the world of the mind and the outer order. It is the secret of the contact that we are after, the point, the moment of the union. We faintly sense the one and we know as faintly the other, but there is a point at which they come together and we can never know the whole of reality until we know these two completely."

Ellen Chesser has such an experience when she sees the mountains of the new region to which her family are moving. It is a complex experience, and she could not possibly have described it to another person. Yet its happening depends not on intellect but on awareness, not on knowledge but on sensitivity. Here is how Miss Roberts describes it: "The mountains grew more definite as she looked back to them, their shapes coming upon her mind as shapes dimly remembered and recognized, as contours burnt forever or carved forever into memory, into all memory. With the first recognition of their fixity came a faint recognition of those structures which seemed everlasting and undiminished within herself, recurring memories, feelings, responses, wonder, worship, all gathered into one final inner motion which might have been called spirit; this gathered with another, an acquired structure, fashioned out of her experience of the past years, out of her passions and the marks put upon her by the passions of others, this structure built up now to its high maturity."

What makes *The Time of Man* a great novel is the extraordinary sense conveyed of Ellen as an almost unseparated part of the tissue of living things, with horses, cows and pigs, and people, beneficent people and hateful people, as if the whole landscape, stretching to the mountains and made up of organisms growing or dying, of corn and grass and animals and humanity and even rocks ("Rocks grow," Ellen's father tells her), were part of a single carpet on the earth. Ultimately this continuity is sensed in time as well as material. Jasper Kent seems to move into Ellen's life just where Jonas Prather has left off, so that both men, without in the least losing their individuality, seem at times simply to express the male aspect of nature. Similarly Ellen, in the end, feels that her life is so innately an extension of her mother's that she can share her mother's memories: "Going about the rough barnlot of the farm above Rock Creek, calling in the hens, breaking them corn, Ellen would merge with Nellie in the long memory she had of her from the time when she had called from the fence with so much prettiness, through the numberless places she had lived or stayed and the pain she had known, until her mother's life merged into her own and she could scarcely divide the one from the other, both flowing continuously and mounting."

There is none of the solemn hymning to the land in *The Time of Man* that we find in Ellen Glasgow and Willa Cather. That was to appear in her fiction soon enough, but in the beginning she was free of it. Campbell and Foster point out the interesting twist that Miss Roberts gave to the philosophy of Bishop Berkeley which she had adopted for her own: "For Miss Roberts indeed there is no contrast between knowledge of the earthy and that of the spiritual; epistemologically, the two were the same for her, as they were for Berkeley, but the emphasis of the artist and her philosophical master, as might be expected, is different: whereas Berkeley as a philosopher is engaged in transforming what is called the physical into that on which it is dependent for its existence, the spiritual, Miss Roberts as an artist seems at one level to be transforming the spiritual into the physical, the sensuous."

But the sensuous has far greater significance in her work than it does in that of an ordinary realist. As Miss Roberts put it herself: "We go into the unseen by way of the visible, into the unknown by way of the known, into nous by way of the flesh and the dust."

The first symptoms of the attenuation of power which Emily Brontë escaped are observable in her very next book, *My Heart and My Flesh* (1927), which introduced the theme that she was to work over and over in the next years: the baffled, humiliated, at times actually violated heroine, after a volume of sleepwalking and groping, punctuated with nightmares, finds a spiritual rebirth in the arms of a strong man who has remained close enough to the soil to be uncorrupted. It is the ancient legend of death, burial, and rebirth, but that is no excuse for solemnity that is always verging on the tedious. Theodosia Bell, the heroine of *My Heart and My Flesh*, suffers two shocks amounting to traumatic experiences: she is brutally deserted by her lover who, overnight, and without even a decent shadow of subterfuge, turns his ardor to another girl, and she discovers that her dissolute father is also the parent of three Negroes, two girls by one woman and a half-witted boy by a second. In an effort to discover her own identity, which has become confused in her mind as a result of these new relationships, she befriends the Negro girls. When the older one murders her lover and the younger sleeps with the idiot brother, Theodosia becomes unbalanced and goes off to live in the country with a crazy aunt who half-starves her. Rescued by the local doctor, she recovers and regains her mental and physical health in a simple rustic atmosphere and with the admiration of a fundamental man. In Caleb Burns, the farmer, "there was a sense of the whole country, of the rolling farms as owned up and down the watercourses and farther, including the town, Anneville and beyond, other towns, Lester, Quincy, all the reach of the entire region."

Miss Roberts' solution of a reconciliation with natural things is expressed in the final paragraph, where Caleb wanders about the farm at night: "The leaves of the poplar tree lifted and turned, swayed outward and all quivered together, holding the night coolness. The steps returned to the pasture, going unevenly and stopping, going again, restless. They went across the hollow place and came back again toward the rise where the cows lay. They walked among the sleeping cows, but these did not stir for it was a tread they knew."

Glenway Wescott wrote a description of Miss Roberts at this period (1927–28) which may give a clue to what was happening to her writing. She had a patrician aloofness, "something blue-blooded, almost Russian, in her bearing," like one of "antique gentry brought low." "I saw her . . . down one of those wild New York streets scarcely occidental in mood, where the workers go half-naked and negro boys throw balls . . . in a darkened, hot but never warming room, seated with her yellow-crowned head bowed almost between her knees as are figures in certain Blake drawings; now signalling from the window with a towel when she had need of human attendance, now like royalty in a convent drawing apart in an arrogant and pious self-communion; abstractions forming out of the tedium, the shadows of past persons becoming the flesh of future characters — thinking, thinking, remembering, biding her time, uttering extensive, dreamy theories and troubling witticisms, with an occasional incorrectness of folk-songs in her speech."

She laughed so hard in reading the manuscript of *Jingling in the Wind* aloud to a friend that she had to stop reading. Such remoteness from others and enchantment with self can have disastrous results on art that must, in the last analysis, be communicated. At the same time Miss Roberts was becoming the most extreme of valetudinarians. She went in now for every kind of fad, believing that the sun was a cure-all, carrying her own drinking water, checking on the temperature of her dentist's office before she would make an appointment. A neurotic can perfectly well be a literary genius, but his greatest danger is always that he will not recognize when he is dull.

Jingling in the Wind (1928) is one of the dullest novels ever written by a first-rank American novelist. Its allegorical character may remove the need for flesh and blood in its people, but allegories should be very sharp and very funny, and it is neither. Jeremy and Tulip, as rainmakers, represent the synthetic, half-baked modern world that cannot wait for the clouds to supply water but must set up machinery to precipitate the precipitations. The novel is shrill and silly, like the later fiction of Edith Wharton, in its denunciation of the cheapness of contemporary American life. The only way that Miss Roberts could demonstrate what America had lost was to show, not what America was, but what America had been, and this, with much happier results, she accomplished in *The Great Meadow* (1930).

After *The Time of Man*, it is the best of her novels. It is inferior only in that it shows the hymnal quality of which *The Time of Man* is so happily free. Miss Roberts makes it only too clear that she is celebrating the courage and the endurance of the first settlers of Kentucky; Daniel Boone himself is one of the characters. Diony Hall and Berk Jarvis, with their silent understanding and deep love of each other, with their unflinching heroism and dedication to the development of a new land, might be figures in a mural of pioneers in a post office. But having said this, let one try to rob the statement of some of its denigration by insisting that it is a *good* mural. The pace of the story is slow until Diony and Berk arrive at Fort Harrod, but thereafter it is tensely exciting. The murder of Berk's mother by Indians, his leaving his wife and child in a dogged, solitary pursuit of revenge, his long absence and ultimate return, a sullen, possessive Enoch Arden, to take back his wife from another, is as gripping a tale as exists in the fiction of the American frontier.

As in *The Time of Man* the characters are a part of the land which they love and for which they have abandoned the relative ease of Virginia. Diony is a magnificent study of a frontier woman. She loves Berk passionately and tries to persuade herself that he is living long after the rest of the stockade community take for granted that he is dead, but there is no place in that primitive world for a young woman without a man, and her economic need for a second husband is soon enough followed by the pricking of her physical desire for one. Such infidelity would be scarcely imaginable among the embittered heroines of Ellen Glasgow. Diony's abandonment of her interim husband to return to Berk when he reappears at Fort Harrod makes a remarkably effective ending. Few indeed are the writers who could carry it off without impairing the epic quality of the saga. But Miss Roberts, it should be emphasized, was a good poet as well as a good novelist, and the only writer considered in this volume who was.

"*The Time of Man* was my *Hamlet,*" Miss Roberts wrote; "*Jingling in the Wind* was my *Midsummer-Night's Dream* and *The Great Meadow* was my *Romeo and Juliet.*" But *A Buried Treasure* (1931) seems to belong more to the dramaturgy of our own time. It is a dreary little tale, once more allegorical, full of fantastic characters who foreshadow the world of Tennessee Williams and Carson McCullers. Andy and Philly Blair, the old couple who dig up a pail of gold coins and bury it again in fear of robbers, Ben Shepherd who comes to town to transcribe the dates of his ancestors from the tombs in the cemetery and finds a bone of one which he carries about in his pocket, a hen that eats her own eggs, a father who claims that his daughter is illegally married in order to get her

home to be his cook — we begin to recognize the whimsical southern cast that has fascinated later audiences. But they fail to come
alive.

The Haunted Mirror (1932) is a collection of short stories, one
of which, "The Sacrifice of the Maidens," about a young boy watching the ceremony in which his sister becomes a nun, plays up a
fascinating conflict of pagan and Christian values, but it was written before *The Time of Man. He Sent Forth a Raven* (1935),
written in this later period, is another allegorical novel, this time
a dark one, with a World War I setting. Stoner Drake vows that he
will never set foot on the soil if his second wife dies, and she does,
and he executes his oath by staying indoors for the rest of his days.
He gathers about him a group of loquacious characters who represent the folly of a mechanical world at war, who have lost their
connections with simplicity, with nature, with God. The plot seems
to offer diversions and possibilities: the crazy old Lear whose granddaughter, Jocelle, brutally raped by a cousin, at last finds peace and
hope in marriage to the good, simple man who takes over the operation of Lear's farm; but it is very tediously worked out.

In the three years preceding publication of *He Sent Forth a
Raven* Miss Roberts' health had been deteriorating, and in 1936
a specialist finally diagnosed her ailment as Hodgkin's disease. The
remaining five years of her life were spent in a struggle with an
enemy that she knew must win. It was in this shadow that she wrote
Black Is My Truelove's Hair (1938), and her genius, no longer
distracted by the irritants of modern society, went back again to
work for her almost as effectively as in the beginning. Her last
novel is a rich, ordered, beautiful symphonic piece of writing which
gives a fine satisfaction to the careful reader, though at moments
some of the vividness of the characterizations may seem sacrificed
to the symbolism.

Dena Janes, before the novel opens, has run off from her native
village, Henrytown, with a truck driver, Langtry, a dark, dangerous,
tattooed man who symbolizes the empty world of nervous motion
that exists beyond the rural areas. As soon as she has discovered
what a terrible man her seducer is, she has told him that she will

return home, but he has warned her that if he ever hears of her going with another man he will hunt her down and shoot her. In the first chapter we see Dena, distraught with terror at the threat, hurrying back to Henrytown where she is only too grateful to be put up by her sister Fronia, older, twice-widowed, domineering, and to do the chores. The local girls are friendly, even chatty, but it is entirely understood that she is disgraced and "different," and the men either avoid her altogether or ogle and leer at her as a loose woman. Dena, however, does not mind this; there may even be safety in her semi-ostracism. She does her work and diverts herself by taking long sunbaths, naked, behind the house. It is a passive half-life with a certain sluggish peace, better, at any rate, than the hell that Langtry offered.

Life, however, will not allow Dena to escape. Fronia loses a gold thimble given her by a former lover, an obvious sex symbol, and frantically hunts it high and low, even threatening to kill her favorite goose and search for the lost object in its gizzard. Dena, younger and sexually ready, finds the thimble, but before she can give it to Fronia it is stolen by a little boy who sells it to Cam Elliot, the beautiful but shy farm lad, the perfect mate. It is the instrument of fate that draws them together, and Dena and Cam become engaged, but when the banns are published Langtry returns. Dena has now acquired courage and confidence; after a first brief panic, when she tries to hide from him, and he shoots at her and misses, she confronts her former lover boldly and challenges him to do what he must. He repents, and a brave future is left for Dena and Cam. As one can see from this outline, despite the subtlety of the novel's symbolism — its squawking geese, its haunting night cries, its old horses and its new cars — it veers close in the end to the hammy. Yet it never quite reaches that point; that is precisely its artistry. It leaves one with a sense of unity and concord, of nature disturbed and put in order again.

The reviewers felt that *Black Is My Truelove's Hair* was good, but not as good as *The Time of Man*. Poor Miss Roberts learned what so many authors have learned: that a masterpiece is not always a friend. "Would I want to write *The Time of Man* over and over, or even once again?" she protested. But her energy was now running out. The planned epic play for stage and radio on Daniel Boone had to be abandoned. She died in Florida early in 1941.

In the last year of her life she put together the little volume of short stories, *Not by Strange Gods*, that appeared almost simultaneously with her death. Two of these shine with all of her early brilliance.

"The Haunted Palace" is an eerie sketch of poor farmers who move their sheep into the great rooms of a deserted mansion. The wife routs what she believes to be the ghost of the old aristocrat, "the creature or the thing," moving among the sheep with a club and a light, by striking at it, and so shatters the great mirror. It is, of course, her own reflection that she has seen, but she does not know this and is now at ease, and she and her husband count the new lambs born that night and are "pleased with the number they had counted."

"The Betrothed" is a wonderful psychological study, seen from inside the mind of Rhody, of her doubts and panics at the prospect of impending marriage to the man she loves. Her old grandmother gives her a desperate shock by reading her fortune in the entrails of a hog: "She prodded into the wet and bloody mass, muttering. It would be thus and thus, she said. The beast, turned wrong side out, danced still his life dance, blood having run into pans on the ground. Life sat, as a dismembered bird, in the vat of the entrails, still throbbing within itself. You are thus and thus, the grandmother said. . . . She would begin a story of mortality, of bloody bearings, the origin of life acting thus alone in a tub of entrails. She leaned over the mass muttering, the mole on her chin beating lightly with the working of her mouth, it uttering jaunty prophecies of blood. For a moment Rhody wanted to push the old one into the tub of quivering intestines, to thrust her forward and downward into the medium of blood and fat."

Overcome with revulsion, Rhody leaves home to visit her married sister, determined to break off the match. She finds herself an upsetting element in an already tense marriage. Joe, her brother-in-law, is attracted to her, and there are ugly scenes. Rhody flees home and discovers at last that she truly loves her betrothed, Kirk Brown, when her younger sisters burn a letter from him which she has not opened. " 'Me and you, Rhody,' that's what it says in the letter," they jeer. And then everything is all right again. "Life seemed very simple to her when Kirk was near, as if only those things of which he took account had reason or being. Now value was thus focused at the point where his hand closed upon her own, and as he walked he looked at her continually."

Nature can be a nightmare, as when an old witch of a woman grubs in a pig's entrails, or a sister sleeps with her idiot half-brother, or a man commits rape, but peace can follow nightmare if a proper adjustment is made between man and his natural physical environment. What is hard to understand is why the form of the short story did not strike Miss Roberts as a better tool for her purpose than the allegorical novel. "The Betrothed" expresses all that *My Heart and My Flesh* attempts to say.

Still, Elizabeth Madox Roberts accomplished in the best of her fiction, long and short, the object that she set for herself, which should keep her name permanently in the front rank of American novelists: "If I can, in art, bring the physical world before the mind with a greater closeness, richer immediacy than before, so that mind rushes out to the very edge of sense — then mind turns about and sees itself mirrored within itself."

6

KATHERINE ANNE PORTER

KATHERINE ANNE PORTER has been identified with the South and with Mexico; one has even seen her labeled as a "regional writer"; but since "The Leaning Tower" and *Ship of Fools* it should be clear to all that she belongs to the world, or perhaps the world to her. As a novelist, she can no longer be identified with any one state or even with any one country, nor has she any obvious literary ancestor. In another author such lacks might be regarded as limitations; in a great talent they are indicia of what has been transcended.

"I spend my life thinking about technique, method, style," she once told Glenway Wescott. "The only time I do not think about them at all is when I am writing." She is not concerned with the surface aspects of technique that have absorbed so many writers since Henry James. She does not hesitate to be the omniscient author in *Ship of Fools* and to jump in and out of her characters at will. When she is concerned with "technique, method, style," it is with the very guts of fiction: the re-creation of the world and the removal of the author. At least to some of us *Ship of Fools* is a perfect novel, and Miss Porter is the American Flaubert.

Many of her early tales (the first one appeared in 1922) are seen from the point of view of a "Miranda" who corresponds closely

136

to the author. It is like Miss Porter to have started with the most basic element in storytelling: the world and the family as they appeared to a child. They are brief sketches, clear and unsentimental; they say the essential with a minimum of incident. Nannie, Miranda's grandmother's oldest colored servant and former slave, has spent a lifetime serving the family; she has even been married lovelessly to Uncle Jimbilly to suit the convenience of her owners. When she is too old to work any more, she asks for a little cottage of her own on the place which is promptly supplied her. What is her attitude toward these grateful, loving, exploiting people whose care has occupied her entire existence? Indifference. To Uncle Jimbilly, the great-grandfather of her great-grandchildren? Simple indifference. She will not let him share the cabin. "I've served my time," she merely mumbles; "I've done my do, and dat's all." "The Last Leaf" is an unforgettable picture of inertia, of release, of old age.

The early stories were not all about Miranda. "María Concepción" is a cool, bright study of Mexican peasants, showing neither disapproval nor admiration for their primitive ferocity. There they are, as vivid as art can make them; the reader supplies the point of view. We see María in the beginning, married, pregnant, and totally happy. That is the peasant in her: she wants very little, but achieving it, she achieves a complete content that is unknown in the world above her. Juan abandons her for another woman; she loses her baby; and she now becomes as totally wretched as she was formerly totally happy. When Juan returns, flaunting his new woman and child, María murders the woman, adopts the child, and recaptures Juan. The entire village conspires to block the feeble processes of justice, and María goes free, secure in the possession of Juan who ruefully acknowledges to himself that he has at last been worsted and captured by a woman. Four decades before the publication of Robert Ardrey's *African Genesis* Miss Porter understood that, at least on the primitive level, it is the female who must fight to obtain her male.

She had grasped the unself-consciousness of the Latin American, and she was later to make great use of it in *Ship of Fools*. Her

Mexicans, Cubans, and Spaniards behave with the ease and natural grace of cats. They are just as contented, just as beautiful, just as horrible as their feline counterparts. "Flowering Judas" is a study of the utter irrelevance, even malevolence, of the northern reformer in their midst: of the terrible dry Laura, the implacable Yankee virgin who works for communism because she wants to destroy the world. Miss Porter was from the beginning so totally an artist that she escaped the social fetishes of the 1930's. None of her stories of that period seem in the least dated today.

She did not make her first trip to Europe until after her fortieth year. This might seem curious in so international a novelist, but she has explained how much of the old world there was in her new: ". . . in my childhood I knew the French-Spanish people in New Orleans and the strange 'Cajans' in small Louisiana towns, with their curious songs and customs and blurred patois; the German colonists in Texas and the Mexicans of the San Antonio country, until it seemed to me that all my life I had lived among people who spoke broken, laboring tongues, who put on with terrible difficulty, yet with such good faith, the ways of the dominant race about them."

She was born in 1890 in Texas, in "soft blackland farming country, full of fruits and flowers and birds," the grandchild, as she liked to put it, of a lost war, with "blood-knowledge of what life can be in a defeated country on the bare bones of privation." Her family were of pioneer stock; her father was descended from a brother of Daniel Boone. She was raised in the Catholic faith, to which she still adheres, and attended convent schools. She supported herself from an early age in a variety of jobs, usually as a hack writer or journalist, and started working in fiction many years before she published her first story. As a reporter in Denver at the end of the first war she caught a severe case of influenza, and after a long illness went to live and recuperate in Mexico. During the disturbed years of the early 1920's she came to know many Mexican artists and revolutionary leaders.

A Guggenheim fellowship enabled her to go to Europe in 1931, and she settled for several years in Paris. After the publication of

Flowering Judas in 1935 (a limited edition had appeared in 1930) she found herself a literary figure and a favorite of the little reviews and progressive colleges. She is probably the "straightest" writer ever to have received such adulation. Her volume of output remained very small but its quality was always of the highest. Not until the publication of *Ship of Fools* in 1962, the novel on which she had labored for twenty years, did she attain a commercial and popular success.

Miss Porter has been married to Eugene Pressly, of the United States Consular Service, and to Albert Erskine, business manager of the *Southern Review*. Both marriages ended in divorce. Glenway Wescott, a lifelong friend, gives this picture of her: "She has . . . a lovely face, of the utmost distinction in the Southern way; moon-flower-pale, never sunburned, perhaps not burnable. She is a small woman, with a fine figure still; sometimes very slender, sometimes not. Her eyes are large, dark, and lustrous, and they are apt to give one fond glances, or teasing merry looks, or occasionally great flashes of conviction or indignation. Her voice is sweet, a little velvety or husky."

She was born at a good time for a writer, for she was old enough, during World War I, to have comprehended the society to which it put an end, and she had achieved her maturity as a writer and thinker before the violence of the depression years which unsettled so many younger authors. She was able in Europe to study the origin and birth of the second war, the analysis of which, in terms of individuals of different nationalities, has occupied much of her thinking ever since. She has lived in so many places and done so many things that it is not surprising that at times in her life legends have grown up about her. As Ray B. West, Jr., put it, speaking of Miss Porter as she appeared to her public in the late 1930's: "Little was known about her personally, and legends accumulated. It was known that she was a beautiful woman and that she had been associated in some way with the film colony in Mexico, and it was rumored that she had been one of the early silent film heroines, perhaps a Mack Sennett bathing beauty. It was said that she moved often from place to place and that she carried with her a huge trunkful of unfinished material that she would not allow to be published because she was not convinced of its value. She was said to have engaged in a love affair with a Mexican revolutionary. She was thought to be ill with some fatal disease. Word did get around that she was working on a long novel and that she had projected a biography of Cotton Mather."

This was in the period following the publication of the three long stories, or short novels, that were later compiled in *Pale Horse, Pale Rider* (1939). They deal with the three themes with which Miss Porter has been most preoccupied: the question of whether the American past (the southern past) had as much of the dignity and romance as it appears to have had ("Old Mortality"); the feeling of nightmare in a senseless present ("Pale Horse, Pale Rider"); and the existence, in past *and* present, of an evil, of an almost ungraspable human malignity that may well be fated to triumph over life itself ("Noon Wine"). We shall see this third theme grow to occupy her fiction to the exclusion of the first and to the curtailment of the second.

The early part of "Old Mortality" beautifully establishes the legend of the romantic South. The young Miranda is enchanted by her family's tradition of Aunt Amy's beauty and charm. Aunt Amy's story, indeed, might have been written by Margaret Mitchell; it is all dancing and passion and duels and early death. Yet Miranda has no personal memory of Aunt Amy. She remembers once meeting Uncle Gabriel, a drunk and a gambler, who has married a shrewish second wife. Yet even this picture has the romance of collapse. What has no romance at all is the light (if it *is* light) shed on the past by her sour old-maid Cousin Eva, whom Miranda, now grown up, encounters on the train coming home to Uncle Gabriel's funeral. In Cousin Eva's version of the legend, Aunt Amy was a giddy and selfish flirt who died of a tuberculosis brought on by "drinking lemon and salt to stop her periods when she wanted to go to dances." Miranda is not convinced that this is a truthful version of what happened, but it goes far to rub out the glamour of the past, and when she sees her father and Cousin Eva, who have nothing in common *but* the past, united in their need to talk about it to the exclusion of Miranda, she understands that she must make her own present, perhaps so that she too may have a past, even ultimately a legend. "It is I who have no place," she reflects."Where are my own people and my own time?"

"Pale Horse, Pale Rider" gives Miranda her own people and her own time, but they turn out to be horrors. The action occurs during World War I, when she is working on a newspaper somewhere in the United States. The vagueness of the site intensifies the nightmare quality of this admirable tale. The influenza epidemic is raging; Miranda contracts the disease, and her lover, Adam, dies of it. The story from the beginning has the feverish atmosphere of illness. The two sinister men who come to Miranda's desk to solicit fifty dollars for a Liberty Bond might be gangsters on a "protection" shakedown. The war hysteria has crazed her world, so that Miranda, untouched by it, feels set apart, a shivering lamb amid bellicose wolves who howl safely, three thousand miles or more from the front. "The audience rose and sang, 'There's a Long, Long Trail A-winding,' their opened mouths black and faces pallid in the reflected footlights; some of the faces grimaced and wept and had shining streaks like snails' tracks on them." Miranda is the one sane person in the asylum; the others have "pulled down the shutters over their minds and their hearts."

Adam, her lover, is free like her, but he is in the army and about to be shipped abroad. He has no need for vicarious thrills. The irony of the story is that he, with all the physical and moral strength that she lacks, the symbol of what the world perhaps once was and perhaps could be again, the Adam of the Garden of Eden, succumbs to the flu that he has caught from her. "Pale horse, pale rider, done take my lover away." She faces the ultimate horror of her loss, so much greater than the horror that she has felt at the nonsense of the home front, with a steadier eye. In the Armistice, in the "dead cold light of tomorrow" there would be time for everything.

"Noon Wine," the masterpiece of the trio, is the story of three men, one an exploiter, one the exploited, and the last a kind of nemesis or devil. Olaf Helton comes to work on Mr. Thompson's ragged little patch of a dairy farm which, by dint of unflagging industry, he restores to a paying condition. Mr. Thompson takes a conscienceless advantage of him and pays him a slave's wage, but the dim-witted Helton is perfectly happy so long as he is left alone in his few hours off to play the same tune over and over on his harmonicas. Only when anyone threatens to touch the latter does he become ugly. Homer T. Hatch, a man who is not fat but who looks as if he "had been fat recently," with brown rabbit teeth and a loud humorless laugh, comes to reclaim Helton for a lunatic asylum, and Mr. Thompson, acting on a sudden wild impulse, fells him with an axe. Helton, running away from the scene, is shot and killed by pursuers, and Mr. Thompson is acquitted on the perjured testimony of his wife who swears that she saw Hatch pull a knife on Helton. Thompson's life thereafter, however, is made unendurable by the neighbors, and at last he kills himself.

Homer T. Hatch is the embodiment of human malice. He spends his life recapturing escaped lunatics, which appears to be his only pleasure. He may be a bit of a lunatic himself, or he may be a symbol of the perversity of human nature. He does what he does for no principle, for no god, not even for revenge; like Javert in *Les Misérables* he enforces the law for the mere sake of enforcing it. Everything, the wretched Thompson tries to persuade himself, would have been all right if Hatch had only stayed away. But Thompson's unprecedented violence in killing Hatch is quite inexplicable to his sons, his wife, his neighbors, and ultimately to himself. He is obsessed with the need to substantiate to everyone his own false version of what happened. In the end he cannot live either with their disbelief or with his own. He *has*, in one fashion, killed Hatch in self-defense, because Hatch in threatening Helton was really threatening him. Thompson knows that his happiness and prosperity have been the work of the simple-minded harmonica player of whom he has taken unscrupulous advantage.

In the perfection of its sinister mood and in its economy of detail, in its unrelieved grimness, this story is the equal of *Ethan Frome*. But the vision of evil suggested by Homer T. Hatch was to be pursued by Miss Porter far beyond the southern dairy farm where he meets his just deserts. To her, as the years went by, national boundaries lost their significance. She found that she did not need, in James's famous phrase, "to be tethered in native pastures." She could embrace the world and use the world. She was to become that rarest of things, a true international novelist. And she was to find Homer T. Hatch in Berlin.

She published "The Leaning Tower" first in the *Southern Review* in 1941, after the war which is fomenting in the story had begun. Miss Porter became increasingly specific about her times and places as her work progressed. The action of *Ship of Fools* occurs on a transatlantic crossing from Veracruz to Bremerhaven, August 22–September 17, 1931, and that of "The Leaning Tower" takes place in Berlin, between Christmas and the end of December in the same year. Hitler is mentioned only once in "The Leaning Tower," and then only indirectly. A barber wants to cut Charles's hair in the long-on-top, clipped-to-the-skin manner of "a little shouting politician" whose photograph is stuck in a corner of the mirror. But the spirit of Hitler is everywhere in the story, which is a sort of advance exercise for *Ship of Fools*. The evil of the voices shrieking at the stumbling clown that haunted Miranda in "The Circus," the wickedness of the parents who try to kill their idiot child in "He," and the deviltry of Homer T. Hatch closing in on the unoffending harmonica player in "Noon Wine," are all to be found in the streets of a depressed Berlin: "There were the faces. Faces with no eyes. And these no-eyes, pale, lightless, were set in faces shriveled as if they were gnawed hollow; or worse, faces sodden in fat with swollen eyelids in which the little no-eyes peered blindly as if all the food, the plates of boiled potatoes and pig's knuckles and cabbage fed to the wallowing body, had weighed it down and had done it no good. The no-eyes in the faces of the women were too ready to shed tears."

Charles, the young American painter, poor by American standards and rich by German, finds himself everywhere resented. When he accidentally breaks the delicate plaster ribs of a tiny model of the Leaning Tower of Pisa, an absurd ornament, as cheap as it is sentimental, he finds that his landlady is anguished. It is to her a precious memento of the better days when she and her husband traveled in Italy, an all too fragile reminder of her own fragile memory of beauty and love in softer climates, happier worlds. Rosa is a bleak Northerner fated to destroy what she cannot enjoy. When Berlin tries to decorate itself, it only makes itself uglier — at least, Rosa's Berlin and the Berlin of her boarders, the silly Heidelberg student nursing his dueling scar and the heavy Bavarian bumpkin studying mathematics. Charles is appalled by the neighborhood: "He drew the lace curtains and saw, in the refracted pallor of the midmorning, winter light, a dozen infant-sized pottery cupids, gross, squat limbed, wanton in posture and vulgarly pink, with scarlet feet and cheeks and backsides, engaged in what appeared to be a perpetual scramble to avoid falling off the steep roof of a house across the street. Charles observed grimly their realistic toe holds among the slate, their clutching fat hands, their imbecile grins. In pouring rain, he thought, they must keep up their senseless play. In snow, their noses would be completely buried. Their behinds were natural victims to the winter winds. And to think that whoever had put them there had meant them to be oh, so whimsical and so amusing, year in, year out."

Charles meets his fellow boarders, and they exchange views. Otto Bussen, the bumpkin, desperate with poverty, makes an unsuccessful attempt to poison himself. The others, Hans von Gehring, the Heidelberg student, and Tadeusz Mey, a Polish pianist, help Charles to revive him. Then they all celebrate New Year's Eve at a cheap nightclub. That is all, but their discussion presages the war that is to come.

Von Gehring wants the war; he looks forward eagerly to Germany's revenge. The mistakes of 1914–18 will not be repeated. Bussen is the German dreamer as opposed to the German militarist; he abhors the idea of carnage, but he recognizes that he will do as he is bid and that von Gehring represents the class that will decide these things for him. Mey, the Pole, perfectly understands that von Gehring and Bussen will destroy him, while all three are united in their hatred of Charles as the representative of that distant rich democracy across the seas, so outrageously and undeservedly immune from the woes and strains of the old world. Yet Charles is far from happy in his immunity. He feels confused and vaguely guilty; like all of his nation he would like to be loved. That night he breathes in the hopelessness of Europe's plight. He sees with despair that there is no arresting all the horror that is bound to erupt from this dull, stale, cold, hungry Berlin with its daily chant of hate. The silly little plastic tower is the symbol of Germany's sentimentalization of a culture that it is about to extinguish.

"The Leaning Tower," which starts magnificently, bogs down a bit in the final discussion. The characters are too obviously representative of nations and ideas; a story has turned into an illustrated lecture, undeniably interesting but still a lecture. But Miss Porter needed practice at the gigantic task that she was setting for herself: to translate into fiction the origins of a world war. Seven days after the fall of France she wrote: "For myself, and I was not alone, all the conscious and recollected years of my life have been lived to this day under the heavy threat of world catastrophe, and most of the energies of my mind and spirit have been spent in the effort to grasp the meaning of those threats, to trace them to their sources and to understand the logic of this majestic and terrible failure of the life of man in the Western world."

She was indeed to trace this failure to its sources, but it was to take her twenty years. She began *Ship of Fools* in 1941 and completed it in 1961. For all its popular success one heard constantly, during the year in which it topped the best seller lists, that it was too gloomy, too saturnine, that there were no "nice" people in it, and that bad as things were, they were not *that* bad. It was sometimes hard to believe that the people making these remarks had lived through an era of human atrocities unparalleled in the recorded history of mankind. It is perfectly true, of course, that war, when it came, produced examples of courage and fortitude as inspiring as the bestiality in Nazi Germany had been depressing, but that was not the subject of Miss Porter's inquiry. She was not tracing what had occurred *after* Hitler challenged the world, but what had produced the challenge.

She had no need to go into the economics of prewar Germany.

She knew that the terrible thing that had happened in the 1930's had happened in the hearts of men. To isolate her examples of these and analyze them she took, as she says in her foreword, the "old and durable and dearly familiar" image of the ship of this world in its voyage to eternity. All of the action takes place on the crossing of the North German Lloyd S.A. *Vera* from Veracruz to Bremerhaven in the summer of 1931. The small first class contains Germans, Americans, Spaniards, Mexicans, Cubans, Swiss, and a Swede. Only the Germans, however, encompass in their group the essential characteristics of their nation. In the steerage are 876 Spanish workers, deported from Cuba to Spain because of the failure of the sugar market. Jammed in below deck in a fetid atmosphere of sweating flesh where seven babies are born on the voyage, they are presented to the reader as a mass, a device which obviously but very successfully simulates the pyramid of the human condition on earth: a huge, poverty-stricken base with a tiny, self-conscious peak. Steerage is never insisted on in the novel; it never becomes a bore; but the reader, like even the most hard-boiled of the first-class passengers, is always uneasily aware that it is there.

Before the *Vera* sails from Veracruz, we are presented, in front of the hotel, with the spectacle of a beggar crawling on his stumps, a poor creature who has been so intricately maimed in preparation for his calling that he hardly resembles a human being. We are never able quite to forget this beggar. He does not come on board, but a hideously deformed hunchback does, and in these two we have always before us the plight of the man whom fate has blasted from the beginning. Miss Porter wants this always to be kept in mind as we learn of the bickering and meanness of the first-class passengers who are dissatisfied with their cabins, their cabin mates, their tables, and their table companions. For she is not one to moan, like a modern playwright, over loneliness and the tragic difficulties of communication. Her characters cannot communicate because they reject communication. They have decided in advance what is due them in the way of honors, friendship, and love, and they have predefined their friends and lovers as persons who must supply their needs. They are not looking for human beings but for fantasies. Consequently they must reject, even hate, the persons who seem to offer friendship or love. But their plight is not really pitiable. Selfishness and egotism are not pitiable. They are funny, and parts of this book are uproariously funny. Miss Porter is never guilty of the sentimentality that masquerades as compassion.

The Huttens and the Baumgartners demonstrate the enormous chasms of misunderstanding which may exist between husband and wife; the Americans David and Jenny show the same between two young people in love. Rieber never succeeds in seducing Lizzi; they hate each other in the end. Mrs. Treadwell fails in her friendships with Freytag and the young officer; Doctor Schumann cannot rise to the demands of his love for the Condesa; the Swiss girl Elsa pines for the Cuban medical student and will not dance with him when he asks her.

Does Katherine Anne Porter, then, not believe in love? Far from it. She has even written that there are more Robert Brownings and Elizabeth Barretts than this world dreams of. It may be precisely to demonstrate that requited and happy love *does* exist, even on the *Vera*, that she introduces the blissful but nameless Mexican honeymooners who never speak or have any contact with the other passengers, but are seen occasionally on deck, hand in hand, with eyes only for each other. Having paid this tribute to Venus, Miss Porter can get on with the real job of the novel, which is to explore the horror that springs from the desperate efforts of human beings to escape the loneliness in which they feel themselves entrapped. As Mrs. Treadwell analyzes the plight of the Baumgartners: "What they were saying to each other was only, *Love me, love me in spite of all! Whether or not I love you, whether I am fit to love, whether you are able to love, even if there is no such thing as love, love me!*"

Yet it should be noted at once that this is not true of all the passengers. It is certainly not true, for example, of the Spanish gypsy dancing troupe. They may be pimps, prostitutes, and thieves; they may be cruel, brutal, and devoid of conscience, but they are not in the least bit lonely. The men force the women to sell their bodies to other passengers, seize the money they earn, and beat them if they suspect them of having derived the least pleasure from this compulsory infidelity. But, beautiful, muscular feline creatures that they are, they have instinctively solved the problem of aloneness on a primitive community level. They are a pack rather than a society and as such constitute an annoyance rather than a threat. The same is true of the Cuban students. But with the Northern races the fretting complications of self-consciousness appear. The Americans Jenny and David, traveling together but not married, provide a sorry study of the devastation that love can reap in a match of incompatibles. Jenny has a generous, outgiving nature, which has attracted David initially but which now embarrasses him cruelly in public. His own common sense and realism operate to fortify the emotional stinginess of his character, which drives Jenny to despair. However, be it observed that David and Jenny, in seeking to lose their loneliness in love, hurt only each other. In their dealings with the other passengers they are the most decent persons on the ship. Jenny may be repulsed and rejected by those whom she seeks to befriend, but at least she is trying to be kind, and that is a rare thing on board the *Vera*.

The largest group of any nationals in first class — at least the largest group of distinct individuals — are the Germans. The three Swiss, the four Americans, the single Swede, do not purport to represent their countries, but the Germans do, and the *Vera*, of course, is a German ship. The captain and crew represent German authority and the German state. At the Captain's table are two businessmen of upper and lower class, a lawyer, a professor, the impoverished widow of an officer who has won the Iron Cross, and a divorcée who is a ladies' garment business executive. Also on board, though not at this table, are a Jewish salesman, a tobacco stand owner, and a dying religious maniac. The best of the lot is the ship's doctor, but like Bussen in "The Leaning Tower" who defers to the militarist, Dr. Schumann is always at the disposal of the Captain. He does not raise his voice in protest against the anti-Semitism at the Captain's table; his attitude is one of passive contempt for his companions. He is the German intellectual, charming, courteous, disciplined, wise — but not a rebel.

The Germans despise each other quite as fiercely as the other passengers do; in fact, they treat their fellow nationals rather worse than the others treat one another. Frau Rittersdorf sweeps poor Frau Schmitt's toilet articles to the floor; the dying Herr Graf is cruelly maltreated by his nephew; the lovebirds, Rieber and Lizzi, maul each other violently; and the conversation at the Captain's table bristles with the exchange of insults. But there is a difference, nonetheless. However much the Germans may hate each other, they hate non-Germans more. When the steerage Spaniards are crowded on board in Havana, Herr Rieber has a suggestion for their better disposition which might have been laughed at in 1931 but could not induce a smile today: "Herr Rieber and Lizzi Spöckenkieker pranced onto the deck, and Lizzi screamed out to little Frau Otto Schmitt, whose tender heart was plainly to be surmised in her soft pink face: 'Oh, what do you think of this dreadful fellow? Can you guess what he just said? I was saying, "Oh, these poor people, what can be done for them?" and this monster' — she gave a kind of whinny between hysteria and indignation — 'he said, "I would do this for them: I would put them all in a big oven and turn on the gas." Oh,' she said weakly, doubling over with laughter, 'isn't that the most original idea you ever heard?' "

The Captain, who regards the antics of the Spanish dancers and the Cuban medical students with abhorrence, is deeply frustrated that he cannot clap them in chains and stick them in the hold. He has fantasies of what he would like to do with a machine gun to the junky piles of humanity that have not been cleansed by German discipline. The terrible thing about Miss Porter's art is that it makes the reader understand and almost sympathize with the heartless Captain. The manners of the Spanish troupe seem at some nightmarish moments offensive enough nearly to justify the worst excesses of dictatorship.

But simple irritation cannot provide a sure enough foundation for the Nazi state. For that hatred is needed, and hatred of a fictitious enemy is more enduring than hatred of a real one, for the danger of pity is obviated. There is only one Jew among the German passengers, Löwenthal, a salesman, and he is simply despised and ignored. The real hatred of the Captain's table is reserved for

Freytag, a fellow German who is *not* a Jew, but who has married one. When this awful fact is discovered, poor Freytag becomes the ideal target. He *looks* like a perfect specimen of the super race: he is handsome, brilliant, upper class, and successful, but once smeared with the dirty brush of prejudice he becomes a mere thing to be trampled on by his erstwhile envious inferiors. And how they love it when they evict him from the privileged table! How it draws them together in the charmed circle of national spite! Miss Porter describes their euphoria in a wonderful passage climaxing the novel:

The ring was closed solidly against all undesirables, ally as well as enemy. All the faces were relaxed with sensual gratification, mingled with deep complacency: they were, after all, themselves and no one else: the powerful, the privileged, the right people. The edge being taken off appetite, they fell to being charming to each other, with elegant gestures, and exaggerated movements of their features, as though they were in a play; making a little festival to celebrate their rediscovered kinship, their special intimate bonds of blood and sympathy. Under the gaze of aliens as they believed — in fact no one, not even the Spaniards, was paying any attention to them — they set an example of how superior persons conduct themselves towards each other. Herr Professor Hutten ordered wine and they exchanged toasts all around. They smacked their lips and said, "*Ja, ja!*"

Even little Frau Schmitt, who had wept when the Captain chastised her publicly, though for her own good, and who suffered at the very thought of the miseries of the world; who wished only to love and to be loved by everybody; who shed tears with sick animals and unhappy children, now felt herself a part of this soothing yet strengthening fellowship.

This is how the Germans solve their problems of loneliness and communication. Ultimately, it will be at the near cost of civilization. Only two things really "happen" on the *Vera*'s trip, in terms of the old-fashioned plot: Freytag is expelled from the Captain's table, and a poor Basque, a wood-carver, is drowned saving the life of an old bulldog that has been cast into the sea by a vicious pair of Spanish children. One can read every kind of significance and religious symbolism into these two events, but it seems fairly clear that they represent in the large man's capacity for malignance and his capacity for self-sacrifice, his cruelty to his fellowman, and his willingness to die — for a bulldog. The act of the Basque is foolish, even crazy, but it awes the ship's company. However they may reject it, however they may sneer, they are uneasily aware that they may have witnessed something fine. It is the one note of hope in the whole long novel, but is it not in fact about the only one we have?

Innovation in the modern novel is often mere trickiness: to eliminate plot, to eliminate time, even, as in some recent French fiction, to eliminate characters. Katherine Anne Porter in *Ship of Fools* has used no tricks that were not contained in the workbag of George Eliot. Her innovations, however, are still fundamental. Her book not only contains no hero or heroine; it contains no character who is either the reader or the author, no character with whom the reader can "identify." Nor is there anywhere in the book any affirmation of the basic striving upwards or even courage of mankind, always considered essential to a "great" novel. To have put it in would have begged the very question the novel asks. And, finally, despite all of Henry James's warnings, Miss Porter has eschewed her "native pastures." Not only does the action take place at sea, between the ports of countries other than the United States, on a German boat, but the American characters are less vivid than the German and Spanish, are even a bit pale beside them. Mrs. Treadwell seems less of a born New Yorker than the Captain seems a Berliner.

Yet the experience of reading *Ship of Fools* is still an exhilarating rather than a somber or depressing one, because Miss Porter has reproduced the very stuff of life in reproducing those twenty-seven days on the *Vera*, and her novel sparkles with vitality and humor. It has been frequently said that the novel form can no longer encompass our times, that they are too vast, too messy, too unbelievable. Yet what are the times but the human beings who live in them, and what has fiction ever treated but human beings? Miss Porter has demonstrated that the seeds of a vast, globe-shaking war can be the material of a great novel published in this decade and read by a public numbered in the hundreds of thousands. It is the best news in fiction that we have heard in many a year.

7

JEAN STAFFORD

SECOND TO HENRY JAMES, Proust was probably the strongest influence on young American novelists of the 1940's and early 1950's. It became the fashion to see his guiding hand in every reference to time and childhood. But when *Boston Adventure* appeared in 1944, it was apparent, to many of us at least, that here was a first novel that caught the very essence of the master's flavor: the continual contrast of a dreamlike childhood, nostalgically recaptured, with a highly vivid, specific study of the more contemporary "great world." Sonia Marburg, one by one, gradually identifies the objects in the fanciful red room, the refuge that her imagination has seemingly created out of a void, with items in her past that she has not, until they spring to mind, consciously remembered, while Miss Pride, a Bostonian Guermantes, is engaged in distinguishing carefully the exact social positions of an Emerson and a Revere.

While the themes are everywhere interrelated, Jean Stafford nonetheless, in dividing her novel into two parts, assigns one to each part. The first deals with Sonia Marburg's childhood at a seaside town near Boston where she works as a chambermaid in a hotel for summer residents; the second, with Boston society in which, through Miss Pride, she at last gains a brief and precarious foothold. The atmosphere of the first chapters admirably conveys the cloudy coldness of a winter beach. The descriptions of the sea and the deserted hotel have the eeriness of Dickens and fit perfectly with the unreality of Sonia's background: her lunatic Russian mother, her German cobbler father, the memories of a Europe that has nothing to do with New England or the gold dome of the distant State House in Boston. Sonia has no life but that of her dreams. She rejects the vulgar world of the Brunsons who employ her to wait on table and chooses for her fantasies the Boston of Miss Pride, the grim old aristocrat whose room at the summer hotel she cleans. Like Marcel in Proust's novels, she has only one ambition, though hers is simpler. He yearns to be a part of the magic world of the Guermantes, and she wants to go to Boston, merely to live in Miss Pride's house. That is all. Love, marriage, children, a career, none of these things matter. If she can attain a room in that house, she will have attained nirvana.

And in the second part of the book she attains precisely that. She learns what she has deep down always known: that there is nothing particularly admirable or even particularly interesting about Miss Pride's circle of blue bloods. Like the Guermantes family they pretend incessantly not to care about the only things they *do* care about: their own birth and position. Hopestill Mather, Miss Pride's beautiful and reckless niece, marries the young doctor who has engaged Sonia's own rather vague affections, but she marries him only because she is pregnant by another man and needs a father for her child. And Miss Pride herself turns out to be a selfish and heartless old woman who pays to put Sonia's mother in a private asylum only to bind Sonia to her as the companion of her long, fretful old age. Yet Sonia has not been entirely the loser in taking this gift borne by the Greeks. In facing Boston she has fought her way out of her own fantasies, and she knows now that she will not lose her sanity as her mother has.

It is difficult to convey a sense of the unique aesthetic appeal of *Boston Adventure*. It is perhaps in the contrast between its dreaminess and its sudden specificity: characters like the Brunsons, large, ugly, wonderfully droll, suddenly emerge, as if out of a fog, to startle and delight. Nathan Kadish, the young Jewish radical, with the purple birthmark on his cheek and the chip on his shoulder, is as vivid as Marcel's friend, Bloch, when he hisses "Slave!" at a Boston butler. And there is hilarity, too, when Sonia, drunk, staggers home and wants to suggest to Miss Pride, awful in the doorway, that she have a nightcap with her. Miss Stafford has a poet's eye for the slang, the slogan, the comically vulgar detail that will suddenly superimpose twentieth-century commercial civilization on the dignity of the ancient past.

Ellen Glasgow found this novel an "endless exercise" and protested that to "anyone who has known Boston and Back Bay, the setting of that adventure is more ludicrous than amusing." Many who profess to have known the old Faubourg Saint-Germain have said as much of Proust. But it must be remembered that we see society in *Boston Adventure* through Sonia's eyes. People forget how constantly they label themselves in their acts and talk, particularly to the Sonias of this world who are looking for labels. Society people invariably maintain that they are interested in everything in the world *but* society; indeed, it is their constant pose that society, in *their* sense of the world, no longer exists. But Proust and Miss Stafford chose not to be contained by this.

She came by her knowledge of Boston honestly enough. In 1940 she married the poet Robert Lowell, a great-grandnephew of James Russell Lowell, and a descendant of Mary Chilton Winslow, who, according to tradition, was the first woman to disembark on Plymouth Rock. But Miss Stafford herself sprang from settlers who had pushed further west. She was born in 1915 in Covina, California, the daughter of John Richard Stafford, a writer of westerns. Her childhood was spent in California and Colorado. After her graduation from the University of Colorado she went abroad to study philology in Heidelberg. Words have always fascinated Miss Stafford as they fascinated Emily Dickinson; both could find infinite edification in reading dictionaries. In 1936 she returned to America to teach English for a year at Stephens College, Missouri, after which she spent a year as secretary of the *Southern Review*. Since then she has devoted the major part of her time to writing, with occasional periods of teaching. She has contributed short stories, book reviews, and nonfiction pieces to a variety of periodicals, but her name today is particularly identified with the *New Yorker*.

Miss Stafford is a constantly surprising person. It would be natural to assume that a woman of such intense sensitivity and intellectual awareness might be vague and otherworldly, or that a woman as dogged by illness as she has been might be deficient in physical vitality. But she is sharply practical as a housekeeper, as a cook, in all the minutiae of life; she can summon a taxi out of air and find a telephone booth in a block where one *knows* there was not one before; and one is constantly amazed at the breadth of her travels and acquaintance. For all the exoticism of her studies and interests, however, she remains firmly rooted in the western soil where she grew up.

Her next novel, *The Mountain Lion* (1947), although using the rich capital of her childhood memories, is not in the least Proustian either in its methods or in the matters which it explores. It is not so much what Molly Fawcett sees or remembers that is significant; it is what Molly *is*, and, incidentally, what she stands for. Molly is a rebellious, moody, exasperating child, precocious, insulting, ugly, pathetic in her desperate rejection of the smothering sexualities of the adult world with whom everyone, even her beloved brother Ralph, even in the end herself, becomes identified. She is a symbol, like the tawny, elusive mountain lion which the men *must* kill, of that virginal, childhood, uncontaminated *something* that is inevitably lost in growing up. In the end she must die with the mountain lion, killed by the bullet that her estranged brother intended for the beast.

Molly and Ralph see the world as divided in two, into what is tiresome and approved of and what is fun and frowned upon. It is the division between the soft and proper, almost suburban, existence of Covina and the hard, bracing ranch life of Colorado, between Grandpa Bonney and Grandpa Kenyon. One of these old men is dead before the novel opens and the other dies in the beginning, yet their specters haunt the book throughout to represent the closed and the open society. Grandpa Kenyon, the beloved, is a "massive, slow-footed bear" of a man, stoop-shouldered, bow-legged, rough of speech and manner, with a whiskey bottle in his scanty luggage, the owner of many ranches, a millionaire, a god. It is inconceivable to Molly and Ralph that he could ever have kissed anyone. After his death his son, Claude, who resembles him, rescues the children temporarily from their stuffy home atmosphere by inviting them to the ranch summers. Grandpa Bonney, on the other hand, is plump, bald, fatuous, the hero of the Victorian parlor, of his widowed daughter, of her Trollopian minister. Yet let it not be assumed that he lacks a lighter side. Miss Stafford has fun with Grandpa Bonney: "What a sport he had been! How full of jokes and pranks! He had always been the merriest one of all at skating parties (to tease the girls he once wore a fascinator to a skating party!) and at wiener roasts, at formal balls and informal Sunday evening chafing-dish suppers. He had had gallant manners with ladies, preserving such customs as kissing their hands and paying them compliments which always contained a word or two of French. What young lady did not delight in having him say to her, 'Mademoiselle's frock is truly *distingué*'? Besides being chivalrous, he could play tricks that were a scream and afterward he would say, 'Forgive me, ladies and gentlemen, but I felt an uncontrollable desire to tickle my risibles.' Once he had put burnt cork all over his face and had pretended to be a darky and his imitation was so good that everyone had been taken in for at least five minutes."

Ralph and Molly passionately elect the Kenyon world, but the tragedy of the novel is that even here, even in the free air of the ranch, the same things will be bound to separate them as in Covina. Eden has a snake; indeed, Molly will not get into a bathtub while the tap is running for fear a snake may swim in with the water. Sex comes to Ralph; he asks Molly to tell him all the dirty words she knows. She repulses him in horror, adding his name to the secret list of people she hates which has swollen to include Uncle Claude and ultimately her whole world. The last name that she pens to it, just before the fatal accident, is "Molly." She dies with the mountain lion because she won't grow up.

The artistic accomplishment of this remarkable novel is that never once does Jean Stafford sentimentalize Molly, despite the fact that she must have a strong feeling of identification with her. We see Molly as unfavorably as do the other characters, biting every hand that tries to feed her, pouring her hate on the just as well as on the unjust. There are even moments when the reader yearns for Molly to behave a bit more humanely, for he has been enchanted by her conduct when she recites her poem "Gravel" to a bored railway conductor, when she sends packages containing thousands of hibernating ladybugs to a science laboratory, when she writes Henry Ford and President Hoover to send her a typewriter. Molly is one of the memorable children of American fiction.

Miss Stafford did not produce her next and (to date) last novel, *The Catherine Wheel*, until 1952. She was divorced from Robert Lowell in 1948 and married to Oliver Jensen, an editor, in 1950. They were divorced in 1953, and in 1959 she married the writer A. J. Liebling. This very happy marriage ended with Mr. Liebling's untimely death in 1964. Miss Stafford is currently working on a new novel which will have a western setting.

The Catherine Wheel, like its two predecessors, has its own peculiar dreamlike atmosphere. The summer colony of Hawthorne, Maine, is composed of lovable, mildly eccentric New Englanders who firmly reject the vulgarity of the present and preserve in their manners and their houses a fine tradition of individuality of taste. Their clinging to better things, to stronger colors, to more dulcet tones gives to the colony a gentle haze of kindliness and irreality, as if wandering up the coast of Maine we had come across survivors from the tales of Sarah Orne Jewett. Katharine Congreve, the beautiful, middle-aged spinster heroine, maintains in all its splendor her father's old white-pillared mansion where she is visited every summer by twin teen-age girls and a twelve-year-old boy, Andrew, children of her first cousin, Maeve, and of Maeve's husband, John Shipley, with whom Katharine has always been secretly in love. This love of Katharine's, like young Andrew Shipley's love for his ugly pal, Victor Smithwick, who deserts him to look after his sick sailor brother, is a Catherine wheel.

The wheel has actually two significations. One is the wheel on which St. Catherine was broken in martyrdom, and the other, derived from it, is the spinning firework, a symbol, as stated in the T. S. Eliot quotation that precedes the book, of illusion. Katharine Congreve has based her life on her love for John Shipley; it is the concealed centerpiece of the ordered and gracious existence of the beloved old maid with her gentle whims and strong generosities and her habits of accumulating curious bibelots and curious friends. Similarly, if more crudely, young Andrew finds joy only in the summer when he can fish and scout the countryside with the abominable Victor. And in the year in which the action of the novel occurs both Katharine and Andrew are shocked out of their habits and fantasies: she by John Shipley's sudden brutal suggestion that he leave his wife and go off with her; he by Victor's complete absorption in the cure of his older brother. Katharine's and Andrew's are the two points of view through whom we gain our knowledge of the other characters and the action.

Andrew is direct; he is, after all, only a child of twelve. He prays to God that Victor's brother may die so that Victor will return to him. Katharine does not go this far on her own account; indeed, she knows that she can never allow Maeve to be deserted. But this has not been her first jealousy of Maeve; in their young days she has resented her own father's preference for Maeve, his niece, and has prayed that Maeve might be scarred for life by a skin disorder. Only Maeve's death, she knows now, would allow her to take John in good conscience. She has sinned, like Andrew, in begrudging one mortal to another, and the two sinners, in their guiltiness, suspect each other. Andrew wonders if Cousin Katharine does not know of his murderous orison, and she is afraid that he may have read his father's letter declaring undying love for her.

The violent ending to this quiet book has been criticized, but it is beautifully prepared by Katharine's ordering of her own tombstone, on which a Catherine wheel has been carved, and by her giving a party for her friends to view it, where only sherry is served. She has renounced John Shipley, and she saves Andrew from the sinful consequences of his prayer by rescuing Victor's brother from an exploding Catherine wheel, but at the cost of her own life. "He was not worth it," she tells Andrew as she expires, meaning his father.

Jean Stafford loves the American landscape and the American past: the Colorado desert, the coast of Maine, the old streets of Boston, Miss Pride picking her way through an ancient graveyard, Katharine Congreve wandering about her father's old mansion. Yet she always sees the relevant modern comment and fits it in exactly. She is very conscious of the deodorant in the drugstore window, the giveaway formality of the *arriviste*, the blue or pink head of the dowager. Her great gift is to be able to place the vulgar detail in the center of the picture without making the picture vulgar, making it, on the contrary, something at once more vivid, faintly humorous, accurate, and at the same time fantastic. What she does to the American scene is to show it as a landscape with a billboard in the center, a billboard that represents the human encroachment on nature, at times funny, at times sordid, at times pathetic, but at all times the reader's and the author's principal concern.

She can find salvation in a detail, a word, a patch of color. Her world is a world of closely observed minutiae. We sometimes have difficulty progressing into a story because our attention is so constantly arrested, and there are times when we may wonder if the parts do not add up to a greater sum than the whole. This may be so in *The Catherine Wheel*, possibly even in *Boston Adventure*, but it is certainly not so in that masterpiece, *The Mountain Lion*.

Only when cruelty or ugliness are absolute does Miss Stafford lose hope. In her terrible short story "The Home Front" she treats a settlement where there is not a detail, a tradition, an artifact to redeem it from the modern wasteland: the hastily thrown together housing development near a war industry in the 1940's. There the bleakness is unrelieved: "Here people lived as headily and impermanently as soldiers on battlefields. There seemed to be no natives unless the babies born here during this long pause could be called such. No indigenous architecture was visible. Probably it existed but it was hidden away behind blocks of temporary structures, by barrack-like apartment houses, sprawling into the yards of churches, huddling in the sulphurous shadows of factories. And although everything was new, made freshly for this especial period in the world's history, it had a second-hand look. Houses, oil drums, buses, people seemed to have been got at a fire sale."

Miss Stafford has written as much fiction in the form of short stories as in novels, and much of it is of the highest order. Best are her character sketches of grotesques, sometimes hideous in their evil, like Persis Brooks, the Bostonian heiress in "A Winter's Tale" who marries a German professor and becomes a Catholic bigot while threatening her Jewish lover with exposure to the Nazis if he betrays her (one must turn to Molière for another such study of hypocrisy); sometimes comical, like Lottie Jump, the little thief in "Bad Characters"; sometimes a pathetic and terrible combination, like Ramona Dunn, the compulsive eater in "The Echo and the Nemesis," whose fantasy is that her lost thin self is a mocking twin.

The themes are apt to be darker than in the novels, and there is a deep concern with pain and with the cruelty that may go into inflicting it. "The Interior Castle" is an unforgettable picture of the anguish of a nose operation without anaesthetic; "The Home Front" tells of a brute of a father who shoots a lodger's adored cat on the suspicion that it has eaten one of his hateful little son's captured birds; "In the Zoo" describes how a dog, brutalized by an old fiend of a woman, savagely kills its former owner's pet monkey. And in "The Maiden" a cultivated German lawyer, happily married to a serenely beautiful woman for twenty years, tells how he had proposed to her after watching the execution of a client.

They are beautiful pieces, almost without exception ("Maggie Meriwether's Rich Experience" and "Beatrice Trueblood's Story" represent an excursion into the lacquered extremism of Elinor Wylie and Ronald Firbank which is decidedly unsuccessful), but they are not on the same level with the novels. This is simply because the particular aesthetic delight of the moods of the latter takes more time to create than a short story can encompass. It is surprising, too, for if one had read the short stories *before* reading the novels, one would probably have concluded that Miss Stafford, mistress of the brief effect, would have difficulty sustaining the longer theme. Yet that is precisely her genius. She is first and foremost a novelist.

8

CARSON McCULLERS

CARSON MCCULLERS had the brilliant and early success that has come to be almost a tradition of the southern school. She was born in Columbus, Georgia, in 1917 of a family that was poorly off, but which sympathized with her early passion for music and writing. She started writing plays in her early teens under the influence of Eugene O'Neill and composed one whose first scene was a graveyard and whose last was a catafalque, on the strength of which her father bought her a typewriter. At seventeen she went to New York to study music at Juilliard with the idea of becoming a concert pianist, but she lost her tuition money in the subway and thereafter supported herself in a variety of jobs, from guarding the door for a near bankrupt comic-book publisher to playing the piano for dancing lessons in a settlement house. Returning from music to literature, at nineteen she sold two stories to *Story* magazine. Then she went back to the South to marry Reeves McCullers (he died in 1953) and lived for two years at Fort Bragg where he was stationed. It was in this period that she wrote *The Heart Is a Lonely Hunter* (1940), whose publication made her immediately famous.

It is extraordinary enough for a first novel, but it is prodigious for an author of twenty-two. Mrs. McCullers, understandably, had not yet learned the tight control of her art that was to make her next book so memorable, but *The Heart Is a Lonely Hunter* embraces all the themes that she was later to deal with more particularly.

The first is loneliness and the seeking of links between lost human beings. To show the quality of reaching out in its essence, Mrs. McCullers selects a relationship between two deaf-mutes, one loving and one indifferent. The indifferent one, Antonapoulos, is half-witted and incapable of the least affection or response. He seems the nadir of the human race. Loathsomely fat, indolent, of childish habits, he sits placidly in bed in his asylum, decked out in all the finery supplied by his adoring friend, Singer. The latter is an example of the principle that love can exist solely in the lover, without any relation to the object loved. But Singer, unlike his crazy friend, attracts the admiring interest of the world which attributes strength and self-sufficiency to his silence. Simply by not speaking, he offers consolation to the Negro Doctor Copeland, who despairs that his children have reverted to the ignorant traditions of their race, to Jake the Communist, who despises humanity, to Mick Kelly, the adolescent girl who seeks adult understanding. Yet Singer himself is more vulnerable than any of them, and when Antonapoulos dies, he can only commit suicide. His strength has been nothing but his love for a freak half-wit locked up in an asylum. This theme was to be more fully explored in *The Ballad of the Sad Café*.

The least successful portion of *The Heart Is a Lonely Hunter* is that which deals with Mick Kelly. It is an advance study for *The Member of the Wedding*, but has little of the brilliant sensitivity of the latter.

Race relations were to be the theme of *Clock without Hands*, but they are more expertly handled in this first book. Dr. Copeland is a dramatic study of the older educated Negro who, after a lifetime of working for the betterment of his race, has the bitterness of seeing his own children accept like dumb brutes the torture of their brother by white prison guards, which results in the loss of his legs. He is driven at last to an unplanned and spontaneous protest and is beaten up himself by police. It is noteworthy that as far back as

1940 Mrs. McCullers should have represented a civil rights worker as organizing a march on Washington and that she should have seen that one of his particular problems would be a Communist who cared more for destroying the social structure than for helping Negroes. Even in the most appalling scenes of violence in the novel there is a strange sweet taste, like that of a sticky soft drink shot with whiskey, or of a kiss ending in a bite, that evokes the nightmare combination of brutality and sentimentality that is so persistent a part of the legend and actuality of the old South.

With the money earned from her first success, Carson McCullers moved to New York which she has always claimed is the best place for a writer. Despite terrible ill health she plunged into the literary life of the city. She called on the "literary exiles" and was soon invited to join a household of esthetes in Brooklyn Heights. There, "sickly, shy and elf-like," in the words of one reporter, she presided over a dinner table whose boarders were W. H. Auden, Louis Mac-Neice, and Benjamin Britten. The walls of this old brownstone were decorated by Pavel Tchelitchew; symphonies were composed at its piano; and the art and musical world trooped through its halls. Somehow in this hectic atmosphere she still managed to write *Reflections in a Golden Eye* (1941).

In a foreword to a later edition of this novel Tennessee Williams speaks of artists and lunatics as existing apart from the generality of readers in a kind of twilight zone where they experience horrors not felt by the rest of humanity. It appears to be his idea that the function of the writer is to send shivers down the backs of the benighted and to give them a titillating taste of the hell from which they have been so fortunate — or so unfortunate (which is the real implication) — as to have been excluded. But this is absurd. Tennessee Williams' fantasies of sex and mayhem are almost universal experiences, which is the reason for his enormous box-office popularity. An artist like Carson McCullers has nothing to do with such ordinary communication. There are certainly horrors in *Reflections in a Golden Eye* that seem to be related to the horrors of Williams' world, as when Captain Penderton stuffs a kitten into a freezing mailbox or Alison Langdon cuts off the nipples of her breasts with a garden shears, but whereas in Williams the horror is the point, in McCullers the horror is a regretted necessity. She slips in her terrible details in a muted, hasty fashion, without dwelling on them; she seems to be saying that she would spare us if she could. But Alison Langdon *did* this shocking thing; that is all there is to it. We shudder and move on.

The remarkable shock effect of this novel is hard to explain. One is tempted to call it, as E. M. Forster called *The Ambassadors*, a "unique aesthetic experience" and let it go at that. But the sense of completion, of catharsis, of the rounding of that perfect circle that begins "An army post in peacetime is a dull place. Things happen, but then they happen over and over again," and ends in the tableau where Captain Penderton slumps against the wall in his wrapper like "a broken and dissipated monk," demands analysis. What has happened to create that effect, *other* than the story of a brilliant, neurotic army officer who has always been attracted by his wife's lovers and who falls at last crazily in love — or in hate — with the almost moronic soldier who watches his wife through the window?

The contrast between man in civilization and man in nature is basic in the novel. The small nervous world of the army post, with its chattering cocktail parties and loveless love affairs, is perched against an undeveloped countryside through which one can ride for miles without encountering another person. Nature surrounds the camp and enters it through Firebird, Mrs. Penderton's magnificent stallion, through Private Williams, in whose eyes there is a mute expression that is found usually in the eyes of animals and who moves "with the silence and agility of a wild creature or a thief," and through Mrs. Penderton herself, a beautiful, easygoing epicurean who is just a bit simple-minded. For Mrs. McCullers is not one to see a "noble savage" in a natural state. Nature in her fiction is apt to be associated with the lunatic and the criminal. Private Williams may strip in the forest and exult in riding bareback under a hot sun, but we know that he has murdered a man.

Alison Langdon, pathetically jealous and alone, Anacleto, her epicene Filipino houseboy, dreaming of ballet, Major Langdon,

causing pain to others in a clumsy selfishness that he only sentimentally regrets, Captain Penderton with his hysteria and frustration, are all in constant conflict with the natural forces outside and
inside themselves. They are reflected in the golden eye of Private
Williams who looks in the window, an eye that does not judge, but
that simply gives them back as they are. That eye is not only nature;
it is death. Penderton, who is afraid of nakedness, both in his wife
and in Williams (who, naked, has encountered the officer in the
forest and rescued Firebird from his whip), takes drugs to induce
sleep. In losing consciousness Penderton imagines that a great dark
bird has alighted on his chest and looked at him with "fierce, golden
eyes." Anacleto pictures to himself a peacock with a golden eye
just before Alison's heart attack.

So, when Penderton shoots Private Williams, to extinguish the
eye that has tormented him to lunacy, it is Penderton who is left
a shaking hulk while in death the soldier still bears the look of
"warm, animal comfort." The gesture of the captain is that of a
child brandishing his fist at a wide, unseeing sky. It has been the
same shrill ineffectiveness with which he has shouted at his mocking
wife and lashed her horse desperately through the forest. The stillness of the ending encompasses the living captain as much as the
dead private.

The Member of the Wedding (1946) and The Ballad of the Sad
Café (1951) represent the art of Carson McCullers at its finest.
One cannot find in the history of the American novella more beautifully plotted pieces. The Member of the Wedding moves steadily
and relentlessly to its shattering final chapter, so that the story effects
in its reader's sensitivity some of the same shock of rebellion and
sudden disillusionment that happens to Frankie Addams. Mrs.
McCullers believes that the crisis of adolescence, the passage from
childhood to maturity, need not necessarily be a gradual one, but
that it may be capsuled into the violent crisis of a single weekend.
Frankie Addams, poised between childhood and maturity, crosses
the line on the eve of her brother's wedding. She wants to escape
from a childhood that has become clumsy, lonely, and grotesque
by the simple expedient of accompanying her brother and sister-

in-law on their honeymoon. At the age of twelve, and despite her size and ungainliness, she has achieved the extraordinary feat, in the sarcastic words of Berenice, the four-times-married cook with the blue glass eye, of falling in love with a wedding. Frankie discusses her rejection of childhood in a series of enchanting scenes in the family kitchen with Berenice and with Frankie's six-year-old cousin, John Henry. Her rebellion explodes at last in four events which follow each other in rapid succession: she has a date with a drunken soldier; she knocks him out with a water jug; she makes a scene at the wedding when her brother will not take her with him; and she tries to run away from home. Then it is all over, suddenly over, and in the last pages, some time later, we see a new Frankie, whom we hardly like, talking airily about Italian art and her new girl friend and desperately hurting the feelings of Berenice who has loved her with such devoted sympathy. Worst of all, she has almost forgotten John Henry who, we learn, has died of meningitis. The sense that the novel conveys of the recuperative powers of childhood at Frankie's age is shocking to the extreme, but as Carson McCullers always manages, with the eerie intimacy of her style, to imply: would one have it otherwise?

The atmosphere of *The Ballad of the Sad Café* is set by one of those sentences that Mrs. McCullers knows so well how to place in the first pages of her books: "If you walk along the main street on an August afternoon there is nothing whatsoever to do." The plot is a perfectly balanced equation; it reminds us of James's *The Ambassadors* where Strether and Newsome change places in the course of the narrative. Amelia Evans, six feet two inches, the man-woman, the rich miser and business executive, taciturn, suspicious, misanthropic, and terrified of sex, cannot comprehend why she has attracted the love of Marvin Macy, the beautiful crook, and although she marries him, she kicks him out of the house when he attempts to make love to her. She, however, is doomed to fall in love with Cousin Lyman, the chattering, indolent gossiping, malicious, yet oddly charming hunchback dwarf, who in his turn falls in love with Marvin Macy, so that the action can only be reconciled in the final appalling fist fight between Amelia and Marvin. The story is a modern version of Racine's *Andromaque* where the cycle of the loved and the unloving can end only in disaster: "For three years she sat out on the front steps every night, alone and silent, looking down the road and waiting. But the hunchback never returned. There were rumors that Marvin Macy used him to climb into windows and steal, and other rumors that Marvin Macy had sold him into a side show. But both these reports were traced back to Merlie Ryan. Nothing true was ever heard of him. It was in the fourth year that Miss Amelia hired a Cheehaw carpenter and had him board up the premises, and there in those closed rooms she has remained ever since."

And then, as the reader contemplates this terrible finale to the simple search for human companionship by three lonely humans, after the moment of awed silence, as in Beethoven's Ninth Symphony, the human voice is suddenly heard in song. The chain gang, seven black and five white boys, produce music that seems to come from the earth itself or the wide sky and that "causes the heart to broaden and the listener to grow cold with ecstasy and fright."

Tennessee Williams, one of Carson McCullers' closest friends, had the insight to see not only that there was a play in *The Member of the Wedding* but that she could write that play alone. Up on Cape Cod one summer he stood over her until she had done it. Produced, it was a splendid success, both critically and financially, but it seemed a final piece of good fortune. She had had a series of strokes in her twenties, and the last one, in her twenty-ninth year, partially incapacitated her. She moved into a large, white Victorian house in Nyack, overlooking the Hudson, and there she has since spent most of her days, in an easy chair in a corner of the living room, with telephone, books, ashtray, and cigarettes close at hand. She reads slowly, mostly books that she has read before.

In 1961, she published *Clock without Hands*, her first book in ten years. It is a curious throwback in form, or rather in lack of form, to *The Heart Is a Lonely Hunter,* and although it possesses many of the individual excellences of her other work, it misses the brilliant writing of the three intervening books. Perhaps this is because, like *The Heart Is a Lonely Hunter*, it is a novel, whereas the other three books are novellas. Mrs. McCullers insisted on the distinction in a letter that she wrote to her publishers asking that *The Member of the Wedding* be described as a novella. "The word *novel* suggests to me a complex work, usually contrapuntal in form, with space for leisure; the novella is deliberately limited, and though there is opportunity for multiple facets and shades of understanding, the novella is single in intention."

Although it is on the authorship of her novellas that Mrs. McCullers' fame will primarily rest, *Clock without Hands* is a memorable book. It makes the mistake of dealing too currently with the segregation problem, so that a sense of newspaper headlines becomes mixed up oddly with the never quite real atmosphere of a McCullers novel, but it is still a vivid picture of the South in the throes of racial crisis. The first sentence, as so frequently in Carson McCullers' books, announces the theme: that death comes to all men but to each man differently. J. T. Malone, the druggist, is dying of leukemia; Judge Fox Clane, in his eighties, with failing mind and body, has little more time than his condemned younger friend; and the old South, with its antebellum traditions of white mastery, is also moribund. Yet there is no fixed moment for the demise of any of them, as there is no fixed period for the enforcement of the Supreme Court's decision against segregation in the schools, which, as announced on the radio in the last chapter, must be eliminated with all deliberate speed. The clock is always there with the warning that time is running out, but there are no hands to tell us how much time is left.

The curious thing about the atmosphere of the novel is that even when it is most sinister, it is humorous and even affectionate. Judge Clane, hugely fat and greedy, loquacious, pompous, absurd, senile, collecting Confederate bills in the hope that they will one day be redeemed, and lobbying for compensation to former slave owners a century after the Civil War, is nonetheless depicted as having a certain magisterial dignity and an old grandfather's lovableness. Mrs. McCullers demonstrates in his affection for the blue-eyed Negro boy, Sherman Pew, that his racial prejudice is theoretical and divorced from his humanity. The ultimate dichotomy of his dotage occurs when he recites the Gettysburg Address in a radio protest against the Supreme Court's decision, a rather crude dramatization of how the South is caught between its love of oratory and high principles and its facts. Similarly, the cop who kills the Negro idiot is immediately sorry for his deed, and the man who hurls the fatal bomb at Sherman Pew can hardly be taken seriously, even by Jester Clane, who seeks to avenge his friend. He takes the murderer up in his plane to kill him, but in the end he brings him safely back to earth. Jester does not like the look of his town from the air, with its avenues and squares so neatly laid out: "As you circle inward, the town itself becomes crazy and complex. You see the secret corners of all the sad back yards. Gray fences, factories, the flat main street. From the air men are shrunken and they have an automatic look, like wound-up dolls. They seem to move mechanically among haphazard miseries. You do not see their eyes. And finally this is intolerable. The whole earth from a great distance means less than one long look into a pair of human eyes. Even the eyes of the enemy."

This paragraph might be Carson McCullers' credo and explains the curious gentleness with which she handles even her cruelest characters. Better them than nothing. Better them than the blank sky. As Oliver Evans put it, the machinery of love is the eternal flaw in Mrs. McCullers' impersonal universe which alone has the power to liberate man from his fate of spiritual isolation.

9

MARY McCARTHY

MARY MCCARTHY'S EARLY YEARS, so poignantly described in her *Memories of a Catholic Girlhood*, were a curious mixture of two extremes: of crowded poverty on the one hand and a stiff, lonely, middle-class luxury on the other. Her parents died of influenza in the 1918 epidemic, leaving Mary, aged six, and three younger brothers to be raised by grandparents. The McCarthys of Minneapolis, rich, prominent Irish Catholics, took the first turn, but instead of keeping the orphans in their own home, they boarded them out with a ghoulish pair of dependent relatives who half-starved and beat the children in a manner worthy of characters of Dickens, later to be young Mary's favorite author. These chapters are the most vivid of the *Memories*, and Lizzie McCarthy, the Pontius Pilate grandmother, "an ugly, severe old woman with a monstrous balcony of a bosom," who "officiated over certain set topics in a colorless singsong, like a priest intoning a Mass," and who lived off the fat of the land while the "spoiled" orphans were despoiled by her fiendish German brother-in-law, is quite as horrible as anything conceived by the author of *Oliver Twist*. Ultimately the children's maternal grandfather, Harold Preston, a distinguished Seattle lawyer, came to the rescue. He sent his grandsons to military school and took Mary home to live with her mother's family.

170

Life now emerged from the Dickensian shadows and took on a more characteristically American appearance, with a convent school and giggling, gossiping girls and dramatic society orations passionately declaimed and daydreams and dates. But she was still basically set apart, a lone child at home in a big silent house, living with grandparents who never entertained and whose disapproval of *all* boys had to be circumvented by subterfuge. Mary McCarthy was cast in the role of observer from the very beginning. The sadistic uncle who forbade her books owes his own survival in fame to the eyes that he thus trained on himself. The role was continued in her Vassar years when she spent her vacations in the homes of classmates and, even when she was living in New York, writing for the *Partisan Review* and espousing the cause of Trotsky, she suffered from a sense of sitting on the benches looking down at the game. "You knew that you were not a violent Trotskyist," Margaret Sargent rebukes herself in "The Genial Host"; "it was just that you were temperamentally attracted to unpopular causes — when you were young it had been the South, the Dauphin, Bonnie Prince Charlie; later it was Debs and now Trotsky that you loved."

The quotation from one of Miss McCarthy's characters to illustrate a statement about her own life is deliberate, for her fiction, like Thomas Wolfe's, is a kind of autobiography. It should be emphasized that this implies no criticism of her fictional method. She has freely admitted that her characters are apt to be drawn carefully from life: "What I really do is take real plums and put them in an imaginary cake." When she sees material at hand that will suit her purpose she sees no need to disguise it, and it would certainly be a waste to put in other people and leave out Mary McCarthy. One might go so far as to suggest that the more directly she makes use of herself as observer and protagonist, the better her literature. Certainly *Memories of a Catholic Girlhood* is unsurpassed by any of her fiction.

Yet curiously enough, considering such frankness in admitting her methods, Miss McCarthy insists in her notes to *Memories of a Catholic Girlhood* on the distinction between fact and fiction. "Luckily, I am writing a memoir and not a work of fiction," she observes, and adds postscripts to each chapter to explain, in rather fatiguing detail, the minute discrepancies between her text and recently uncovered facts of McCarthy history, as if she were a modern commentator scribbling in the margins of some venerable and hitherto unquestioned work. But these very notes betray the fictional essence of the pieces that precede them. " 'Yonder Peasant,' " she maintains, "unlike the chapters that follow, is not really concerned with individuals. It is, primarily, an angry indictment of privilege for its treatment of the underprivileged, a single, breathless, voluble speech on the subject of human indifference," i.e., one adds to oneself, a work of fiction. And as for the chapters that follow, *are* they primarily about individuals? Might one not claim that "A Tin Butterfly" is a study in sadism, that "The Blackguard" is a charming comedy about a little girl's worry over saving the soul of her Protestant grandfather, and that "Yellowstone Park" deals with the disillusionment of a hitherto protected young lady on her first experience with the drugstore clerk, the night automobile ramble, and the bottle of cheap whiskey? One might argue that all of Miss McCarthy's books were fiction or that none of them were, but the argument would be idle. The point is that her vision of our world is a signally enlightening one.

In 1933, after her graduation from Vassar, Miss McCarthy married an actor, Harold Johnsrud. Three years later they were separated. She had herself ambitions to go on the stage, where her brother Kevin later succeeded, but she decided that her talents were insufficient and turned instead to literature. Settling in Greenwich Village, she wrote a drama column for the *Partisan Review* and reviewed books for the *Nation* and the *New Republic*. The Moscow trials disenchanted her with communism, and her marriage in 1938 to the famous critic Edmund Wilson removed her still further from the Bohemian life which she always viewed with a rather ferocious clarity.

Her second marriage also ended in divorce, but not before Mr. Wilson had performed a valuable service to American fiction in persuading his wife that she could write it. In an interview with the *Paris Review* she describes what happened: "Then I married Edmund Wilson, and after we'd been married about a week, he said, 'I think you have a talent for writing fiction.' And he put me in a little room. He didn't literally lock the door, but he said, 'Stay in there!' And I did. I just sat down, and it just came. It was the first story I had ever written, really: the first story in *The Company She Keeps*. Robert Penn Warren published it in the *Southern Review*. And I found myself writing fiction to my great surprise."

Miss McCarthy has said that she regards her first book, *The Company She Keeps* (1942), as a novel, although the idea of putting its stories together as a unit did not occur to her until several had been written. The collection is centered about a fictional counterpart of the author who is called Margaret Sargent in all the stories but the first, where the protagonist is a heartless poseur. In "Portrait of an Intellectual as a Yale Man" the reader sees Margaret through the eyes of Jim Barnett; in the others she appears more directly as "I" or "She" or even "You." She has casual love affairs and serious ones; she damns a Stalinist across the dinner table; she works for a swindling art dealer for whom, out of simple fondness, she performs some dubious errands; she is psychoanalyzed and gets the better of her doctor. But the common denominator, excluding the first story, is in Margaret Sargent's dogged persistence in analyzing and testing her every act and motive under moral laws. So long as she has this awareness, she feels that she has life. "Oh my God," she prays, leaving her analyst's office, "do not let them take this away from me. If the flesh must be blind, let the spirit see." Mary McCarthy's female characters enjoy only in the bleakest fashion the liberties of their emancipated era under the gimlet eye of their own hyperactive consciences. She herself abandoned the consolations of the Catholic faith without gaining the indulgences of atheism.

Like Edith Wharton before her, Miss McCarthy, as a stylist, started at the high level that she has consistently maintained. Her beautifully balanced, perfectly constructed sentences owe much to her early affinity for the Latin tongue and girlhood passion for Caesar and Cicero. "Writing with a Latinate turn," she said, "compressed, analytic, and yet having a certain extravagance or oratorical flourish," was her natural language. The occasional, intentional vulgarisms sometimes have the desired shock effect; at others they are painful, almost intolerable, as when Henry Mulcahy in *The Groves of Academe* takes a seat "still warm from the student's bottom," or when a Vespa "farts" in *The Stones of Florence*. There is a perversity in Mary McCarthy that makes her at moments seem to have to spit in the eye of her admirer, to tear up the scene at which we have been contentedly gazing. It is not Dottie's orgasm in *The Group* or the bedroom scene in "The Man in the Brooks Brothers Shirt" to which one objects; it is the bathroom reference tossed in with the defiance of a naughty child.

It must have seemed at the time as if these long short stories, or novellas, were the perfect medium for Miss McCarthy's talent. Jim Barnett, the "intellectual" Yale man, the self-consciously average (or is it, as the author suggests, anonymous?) American, clean-cut, naive, horribly cheerful, looking happily up at one from an advertised bowl of breakfast cereal, travels in easy, painless, ambling steps from Stalin to Trotsky to Henry Luce where we leave him, prosperous, stout, beginning to drink heavily, and (at last) dissatisfied. Miss McCarthy squeezes out of him all that can possibly be squeezed in her eighty pages; the last drop of his small, sad, mean, uncomprehending soul falls into the final paragraph. This is not so with Mr. Breen in "The Man in the Brooks Brothers Shirt." There is a good deal of him that we do not know, but Margaret Sargent (in both stories the mistress) is here the dominant character, and the subject is her brief but appalling affair with him on a train, which is covered in its fifty allotted pages with an exhaustiveness worthy of Proust.

Miss McCarthy now moved with equal success into longer pieces. In 1949 she published a short satirical novel, *The Oasis*, about a group of politically minded intellectuals, some "purist" and some "realist," the latter being embittered and disillusioned ex-Stalinists who secretly hope for the failure of the group's experiment which is to establish an independent community in an abandoned vacation resort and lead the simple rustic life in protest against a world crazily preparing for nuclear war. Comedy is immediately apparent in what they cannot leave behind: "Agreeing, in principle, that the machine was to be distrusted, they had nevertheless voted to use in their experiment the bicycle, the carpet-sweeper, and the sewing-machine, any machine, in fact, to which a man contributed his own proportionate share of exertion and which tired him like the plough or the hoe. The bath, the flush toilet, all forms of plumbing they tolerated, but they opposed, at least for the time being, the installation of an electric power-plant, proposing to cook by wood and read in the evenings by oil."

The experiment ultimately fails when some neighboring farmers trespass on the community's land to pick strawberries. What is to be done? Are the members justified in excluding other humans? Does it matter that they want their own strawberries for a picnic dessert rather than to sustain life? In evicting the farmers, are they justified in using threats? Force? When one member finally drives them off by brandishing a gun, the community is split into rival sections.

The Oasis would seem more brilliant today if Miss McCarthy had not so far exceeded it in her later novels. It is significant in the direction in which it turned her satire. Ellen Glasgow, Edith Wharton, and Elizabeth Madox Roberts all struck at post-World War I America in the area that Sinclair Lewis hit, Babbittry, but they failed miserably where he succeeded. They had no real sense of what Babbitt was, and Lewis, of course, had more than a dash of him in his own make-up. Miss McCarthy has no difficulty in handling Babbitt; her heroines are even vagrantly drawn to him ("Portrait of the Intellectual as a Yale Man"; "The Man in the Brooks Brothers Shirt"); but she scorns to use her big ammunition against so slow a target. She reserves this for the intellectuals.

She taught English at Bard and at Sarah Lawrence; she knew her "progressive" faculties. She saw that the illness of the modern world might be exposed most effectively by showing its ravaging presence in the very minority who believed themselves most immune. The ineffectiveness of liberal teachers and artists in the twentieth century suggested that their strength had been sapped by the dopes of the chain-store civilization at which they sneered. Where would they be without the ice cubes for the drinks that they had so constantly in hand?

Another book of short stories, however, *Cast a Cold Eye* (1950), was to appear before Miss McCarthy moved on to her major phase. It is chiefly remarkable, aside from the pieces later to be included in *Memories of a Catholic Girlhood*, for a story-essay, "The Friend of the Family," about Francis Cleary, who can come in either sex or even as a couple, the perennial guest, the neutral territory over which the warring wife and husband can temporarily agree. The analysis of Cleary as a dope, as an irritant, and as an ultimate menace is perhaps the most brilliant piece of writing in all of Miss McCarthy's work. One has to have lived single amid married couples to know its uncanny accuracy and its alarming truth.

The Groves of Academe (1952), Mary McCarthy's first full-length novel, represents the apex of her satirical art. It is an admirable accomplishment. We witness, step by slow step, the relentless destruction of a small, disunited, progressive academic world by a monster. Henry Mulcahy, "a tall, soft-bellied, lisping man with a tense, mushroom-white face, rimless bifocals, and graying thin red hair," an apostle of Joyce, Kafka, Proust, and Marx, uxorious, self-pitying, shrill, unscrupulous, perfectly disloyal to the traditions of the past and to the hopes of the future, exuding an atmosphere of domestic confusion, of "children's runny noses and damp bottoms," yet withal a bit of a genius, is the terrible nemesis who alights on the confused campus of Jocelyn College. He borrows from his students; he makes them perform his domestic chores; he does not hesitate to flunk them if they rebel; he neglects his courses; he embroils the other members of the faculty with each other in an elaborate maze of lies. When he is fired, he paralyzes the liberal executive arm by claiming, falsely, that he has been a Communist and is now the victim of a witch hunt. In the end it is the unhappy president of the college who resigns his post, uttering in his despair the cry of Cicero: "How far at length, O Catiline, will you abuse our patience?"

The advantage that Mulcahy has over the other teachers is that his egotism has no flaws. All the rest in this Tower of Babel, however doctrinaire, however pedantic, however bereft of any vestige

of common sense, however, in short, ridiculous, have some minimum of decency, some remnant of idealism, some shadow of hope
that at least *some* student may gain a bit of education at Jocelyn,
and so are vulnerable to Mulcahy who regards the world about him
as simply a stage for the drama of his self-pity. He can fight every
form of progressivism in its own territory because he knows all the
shibboleths and himself believes in nothing. The reader unwillingly
begins to take his side, hypnotized by the charm of his very out-
rageousness. When Alma Fortune resigns from the faculty in protest over his discharge, knowing that she may be forever ditching
her academic career, he gleefully rubs his hands at the prospect
of such a feather in his martyr's cap and promptly ascribes a selfish
motive to her act.

Horrified, fascinated, sincerely troubled in their hearts, the other
members of the faculty endlessly analyze him. Is he mad? Perhaps
he has chosen, like Thomas à Kempis, argues one, to imitate Christ:
". . . by becoming man precisely God underwent what could be
described as madness: the experience of unrecognition fusing with
the knowledge of godhead, the sense of the Message, the Word, the
Seed falling on barren ground." Mulcahy, exulting in his tricks, also
analyzes himself, but he finds a simpler answer. "It was the artist in
him, he presumed, that had taken control and fashioned from newspaper stories and the usual disjunct fragments of personal experience
a persuasive whole which had a figurative truth more impressive
than the data of reality, and hence, he thought, with satisfaction,
truer in the final analysis, more universal in Aristotle's sense." Indeed, this is almost what Miss McCarthy has done herself, for there
are wonderful moments in the novel when, with the dazzle of con-
flicting arguments, Mulcahy seems to be what he claims, when he
works his tricks on the reader as well as on his fellow instructors.

Some critics have asked if a novel can really succeed without
more "heart" than Miss McCarthy appears to have put in this one.
Can it be sustained by sheer intellectual pyrotechnics? But under-
neath all the ridiculous aspect of Jocelyn College, its sloppy, faddy
students, its affectation, its show-off, its arrogance, its ivory towers,
there is still a feeling which comes through to the reader — and which

can come, after all, only from its Juvenalian author — that it is still a place that is intellectually alive. One laughs at the involved discussions between the teachers and the intellectual extremes to which they push each other, but one is interested (a rare thing in fiction) in the ideas expressed as well as the light shed on the characters expressing them. One misses the point of *The Groves of Academe* if one forgets what Miss McCarthy could do with a *nonprogressive* college. There is more sympathy on her part than appears at a first reading for the poor souls struggling for a straw of consistency under the relentless badgering of Henry Mulcahy.

A Charmed Life (1955) continues Mary McCarthy's satirical survey of the intellectual world, changing the scene from the progressive college to a semi-Bohemian community on Cape Cod. This community excludes the local village people, the "natives," and the well-to-do summer folk; it is composed of a little group of would-be artists or critics, living on their dividends or on borrowing, who prefer talk to work and who fear nothing but conventionality, having defined themselves in terms of their own revolt from the rest of American life. Their lack of discipline and coherence has spread to corrupt the village of New Leeds which now exudes an atmosphere of feckless irresponsibility and juvenile self-satisfaction. They lead, these rootless intellectuals and poseurs, charmed lives. Somewhere they subsist, year after year, anesthetized by alcohol, carrying on their interminable arguments, having love affairs with each other's spouses, sleeping off hangovers, and producing their little manuscripts or artifacts. Like the people in *The Oasis,* they depend on the technology of a civilization which they despise; they need deep freezes and canned foods as much as the worst Babbitt in suburbia. Indeed, their only difference seems to be in their dirtier homes. As the heroine exclaims in protest: "This horrible bohemian life you see up here, with lily cups and beards and plastics — it's real leveling, worse than suburbia, where there's a frank competition with your neighbors, to have the newest car or bake the best cakes. I can understand that. I'm like that myself. But here nobody competes, unless there's a secret contest as to who can have the most squalid house and give the worst parties. It gives me the strangest feeling, as if I were the only one left in the world with the desire to excel, as if I were competing, all alone, on an empty stage, without judges or rivals, just myself."

Into this world comes Martha Sinnott, possessed of an "obscure fame" as a play adapter, and her second husband, John, she to write an original play and he to see that she does it. Martha, childless, also wants to become pregnant, and she accomplishes her object, but she fears that her pregnancy may have been caused by her ex-husband, the brilliant and terrible megalomaniac Miles Murphy, to whose renewed attentions she has succumbed after a bibulous party in which the *Bérénice* of Racine has been read aloud.

Of course, anyone else in New Leeds would have let the child be born. John Sinnott need never have known what happened, and, after all, it *might* have been his child. But that is precisely why Martha is not a true member of the New Leeds community. She cares passionately about truth and her own moral position. She knows that it is out of the question for her to give birth to a child of whose paternity she can never be sure. It may seem a curious issue to make, but on it her whole integrity stands and falls. Going to a friend to borrow money for the abortion, she declares her secession from New Leeds:

Her voice rose, in slight hysteria. Warren looked at her in consternation. "Forgive me," she put in. "But it's true. And the whole world is getting like you, like New Leeds. Everybody has to be shown. 'How do you know that?' every moron asks the philosopher when he's told that this is an apple and that is a pear. He pretends to doubt, to be curious. But nobody is really curious because nobody cares what the truth is. As soon as we think something, it occurs to us that the opposite or the contrary might just as well be true. And no one cares."

"Don't you think that's the effect of advertising?" ventured Warren.

Warren, however, gives her the money, and she is killed in a motor accident on her drive home. For by her decision she has taken herself out of the make-believe atmosphere in which the New Leedsians live, and her life is no longer charmed.

The novel, thus, unlike *The Groves of Academe*, is more than a satire. Martha is a heroine who has a moral problem and with whose difficulties the reader can sympathize. But not enough. That is the trouble, and why *The Groves of Academe* is the finer work. Martha's scruples, particularly in view of her lack of them where Miles Murphy is concerned, seem as unreal as all the other worries in New Leeds. It is a bit difficult to see why, if adultery is so lightly accepted, its consequences should be so rigorously denied. Unless Miss McCarthy is saying that Martha had, for the sake of her own compromised integrity, to draw the line *somewhere*. But in all events the problem makes Martha seem a bit remote and shadowy.

Miles Murphy, however, saves the book. He is the one really living character, a magnificent monster who gives the novel some of the vitality that Mulcahy gives to its predecessor. It is tempting to believe that it *was* he who impregnated Martha and that what destroyed the "charm" of New Leeds was this insemination from the real world. He is a horrible great beast of a man, at once intellectual and physical, totally selfish, brilliantly witty, rude, magisterial, unexpectedly charming, and unexpectedly just. Beside him, their natural leader, the other characters seem silly asses. When he and Martha are together, they dominate the conversation as they dominate the book. And, as in all of Mary McCarthy's books, the discussions are fascinating in themselves. This is a sample of Murphy's acumen: "Art historians pretend that it's the philistines that scoff at the new men. Pardon me if I say that's horse shit. The philistines aren't interested in art unless it's called to their attention as something they ought to get sore about. It's the boys and girls with the trained eyes that come to smile at the Armory show and the Salon of the Refusés — the ones who *know* better than the painter. Who laughed at Whistler? Ruskin. Who laughed at Socrates? Aristophanes. Who laughed at Racine? Molière."

Divorced from Edmund Wilson, Miss McCarthy in 1946 married a teacher, Bowden Broadwater. This marriage also ended in divorce, and in 1961 she married a diplomat, James West. After *A Charmed Life* she turned to nonfiction and wrote two remarkable travel books, *Venice Observed* (1956) and *The Stones of Florence* (1959), adding a new color and freshness to subjects that it would have seemed impossible to treat without repetition. Between these books she brought out her masterpiece, *Memories of a Catholic Girlhood* (1957). As she is passionately involved with the hardships and injustices of her own early days and as the persons described are part of her very being, there is a fire and a drive in these memoirs that are not found so strongly in her other books. Charles Rolo has suggested that she reveals herself both as a perfectionist and as a person sharply sensitive to hierarchies, a frustrating combination, for she sees exactly what is first-rate and must feel at the same time, because of the cubbyholing of life, that it is never quite attainable.

By the 1960's, at any rate, Miss McCarthy seemed to have attained almost everything. She was renowned as a critic, both of drama and teaching, as an essayist, as an observer of the current scene from American politics to the ancient cities of Italy, as a wit, as a memoirist, and as a novelist. But she had not had a great popular success, and that was to be hers with the publication of *The Group* in 1963.

She described it in her *Paris Review* interview as a novel about the idea of progress in the feminine sphere, or rather the history of the loss of faith in progress: "You know, home economics, architecture, domestic technology, contraception, child-bearing, the study of technology in the home, in the play-pen, in the bed." And, to a great extent, she has accomplished her purpose. *The Group* is an encyclopedia of the mannerisms, the fads, the affectations of an era. The trouble with Miss McCarthy's method in this book is the trouble with John O'Hara's in all of his: that in an era whose chief social phenomenon is the amalgamation of classes, where hierarchies collapse before the chain store and supermarket, the proliferation of details about any one group (unless it has set itself rigidly apart) does not necessarily illuminate one's understanding of it. In *A Charmed Life* and *The Groves of Academe* Miss McCarthy is dealing with vociferous minorities who care passionately about preserving their minority status. The details of their daily living are so many flags gallantly, comically, and ultimately unsuccessfully raised in the battle against uniformity. But eight Vassar girls of the Class of 1933 are not distinctively different in their tastes and choices from any other eight American college girls. Indeed their depression-born sense of guilt, their need not to be "different," certainly not superior, makes them adopt a sort of economic protective coloration.

But perhaps this is precisely what Miss McCarthy is trying to demonstrate: that "progress" has made us all one and a sorry blend, at that. Every young woman in the 1930's had to deal with sexual freedom and the remnants of the Victorian conscience, with the idea of communism and the memory of *laissez-faire*, with modern gadgetry and the specter of human dignity. If that is the case, Miss McCarthy could have spared us the tedium of some of her inventories. What, for example, do the following minutiae really add to our picture of Helena Davison, whose relentless energy has already been stated: "She could write a severe little essay, imitate birdcalls, ring chimes, and play lacrosse as well as chess, checkers, mahjongg, parcheesi, anagrams, dominoes, slapjack, pounce, rummy, whist, bridge, and cribbage. She knew most of the hymns in the Episcopal and Presbyterian hymnbooks by heart. She had had dancing lessons, ballroom, classical, and tap. She had done field walks in Geology and visited the State Asylum for the Insane, bunked in the Outing Cabin, and looked over the printing presses of the *Dutchess County Sentinel* in Poughkeepsie."

The description continues even after the above, but it has no more significance than the long list of periodicals, supplied in full, to which Helena's parents subscribe. Is the failure of the picture a failure in the author's power of selectivity or in the significance of modern details? It is hard to say. Edith Wharton, writing of a still hierarchical time in *The Age of Innocence*, was able perfectly to suggest the personalities of the widowed Mrs. Archer and her maiden daughter by supplying a few details of their daily existence. They "cultivated ferns in Wardian cases, made macramé lace and wool embroidery on linen, collected American Revolutionary glazed ware, subscribed to *Good Words*, and read Ouida's novels for the sake of the Italian atmosphere."

The real rocks on which the crafts of the Vassar girls founder are not the confusions of twentieth-century progress but the cruelties of twentieth-century men. Perhaps Miss McCarthy believes that

one brings on the other. At any rate, one must turn back to the
novels of Ellen Glasgow for a greater collection of cads than that
which lies in wait for Vassar '33. Kay marries a confused and malig-
nant bisexual who drives her to suicide; Dottie falls in love with a
neurotic whose rigid separation of the physical and sentimental pro-
hibits even a kiss after sexual intercourse; Priss is wed to a Spartan
doctor who carries his fundamental principles to the point of near
sadism; Norine's husband is impotent; Libby's ski instructor tries
to rape her; Polly's lover wants only to obey his analyst and return
to his estranged wife. The only decent man in the novel is Polly's
eventual husband, Dr. Ridgeley, who seems not quite real, being
the *deus ex machina* who solves all her problems by *wanting* to live
with her crazy old father. Lakey's surrender to the Lesbian persuasion seems understandable in the light of what she has seen happen
to the others. The men are selfish, malicious, loveless, and obsessed
with their own psychological problems. With all due allowance for
the trials to young men in depression days it still seems that Miss
McCarthy has stacked the cards against her group. Perhaps the
trouble is that, as she has suggested, her women are all essentially
comic characters, while her men are not. It is as if she had married
Beatrice not to Benedick but to Iago.

All of which is not to say that *The Group* does not contain
some of Miss McCarthy's most entertaining writing. The chapter
where she comes nearest to accomplishing her expressed purpose, where her satire is at its most devastating, is that in which
Priss, dominated by her narrow-minded and doctrinaire doctor husband, reluctantly tries to feed her baby from the breast. The phoni-
ness of the cult of the natural in an age that has lost sight of nature
is nicely caught in the screaming protests of the infant who is trying
to adjust himself to the crazy world into which he has been born.
"In reality, what she had been doing was horrid, and right now,
in the nursery, a baby's voice was rising to tell her so — the voice,
in fact, that she had been refusing to listen to, though she had
heard it for at least a week. It was making a natural request, in
this day and age; it was asking for a bottle."

Although Miss McCarthy shifts the recording point of view from character to character and speaks as the omniscient author whenever she chooses, she elects to leave the reader in some slight doubt as to whether Kay in the end dies of her own volition or by accident. Perhaps she was not entirely sure herself. Kay and Harald analyze each other fiercely and cleverly throughout the book. He, as the survivor, is given the last word on his way to the cemetery when he suggests to Lakey that Kay killed herself to prove her superiority to him, who had tried several times abortively. One is never sure, just as one is not sure of the validity of any of the many fascinating theories that they spin about each other. One is sure only of the fact that there is no love between them, and that there never has been. They are terrible examples of their time, two scorpions in a bottle, lashing at each other in the endless jargon of their Freudian speculations. Kay is morally superior, like all Miss McCarthy's heroines, for she will at least admit the egoism that lurks behind her every act — in fact she will invent it if it is not there. Harald, the McCarthy male, simply sweeps the trash of his utter selfishness under the rug of a factitious psychological personality.

The accomplishment of the book is that even where it verges on the tedious, it is the tediousness of mid-twentieth-century life where the colors of the past blend into a dull brown in the electric mixer of modern technological civilization. It will be interesting to see where Miss McCarthy goes from here.

She has her doubts about the novel. She wrote in "The Fact in Fiction" that it has always been concerned with fact (*vide* the huge, detailed social backgrounds of the nineteenth-century novelists) and that in our own world fact, i.e. Buchenwald and Auschwitz, the population curve of China and the hydrogen bomb, has become too improbable. "It would seem," she argued, "that the novel, with its common sense, is of all forms the least adapted to encompass the modern world, whose leading characteristic is irreality." Proceeding in "Characters in Fiction" from what the novel is up against to the disease within the modern novel itself, she laments the loss of the hero and the substitution of consciousnesses totally alien to the author himself. She seems to see the modern novelist as a kind of monologist, a Ruth Draper, changing her personality with her hat or scarf, now hobbling like an old woman, now bounding about the stage like a Diana. She even criticizes her own creation of Henry Mulcahy: "There is something burglarious about these silent entries into a private and alien consciousness. Or so I feel when I do it myself. It is exhilarating but not altogether honest to make believe I am a devious red-haired man professor with bad breath and bits of toilet paper on his face . . ."

When the Victorian reader read *David Copperfield* or *Jane Eyre*, he knew that Dickens was behind the hero of one and Charlotte Brontë behind the heroine of the other. This is no longer the case in modern fiction. "What has been lost . . . is the power of the author to speak in his own voice or through the undisguised voice of an alter ego, the hero, at once a known and an unknown, a bearer of human freedom."

It is not clear why Miss McCarthy, nurtured on Catullus and Juvenal, should feel limited by the modern novel as defined by any writer other than herself. One sees no reason why she should not speak in a new novel through the undisguised voice of an alter ego. Perhaps she will. She said in her *Paris Review* interview that Pasternak had been able to do it in *Doctor Zhivago* because he was unaware that Joyce and Faulkner had removed the author (and hence the hero) from the novel! She would like now to restore the author, not in the disguise of her heroine, but in some other fashion not yet determined. All that she is sure of is that the technical development of the novel, begun by Flaubert and James, has been "absolutely killing" to it. The problem of the point of view has been solved by a species of ventriloquism. This was a discovery that she made when she returned to nonfiction: "The reason that I enjoyed doing those books on Italy, the Venice and Florence books, was that I was writing *in my own voice*. One book was in the first person, and one was completely objective, but it doesn't make any difference. I felt, you know, now I can talk freely! The books were written very fast, the Venice one faster. Even the Florence book, with masses of research in it, was written very fast, with a great deal of energy, with a kind of liberated energy. And without the peculiar kind of painstakingness that's involved in the dramatization that one does in a novel, that is, when nothing can come in that hasn't been perceived through a character. The technical difficulties are so great, in projecting yourself, in feigning an alien consciousness, that too much energy gets lost, I think, in the masquerade. And I think this is not only true of me."

Mary McCarthy's own voice is heard more in all of her work than she is perhaps aware of. Yet in this interview she appears to recognize that the more it is heard, the better her writing. Certainly the more it is heard, the more feeling there is. One hates to say it, because one hates even by the remotest implication to seem to abandon fiction to the breast-beating writers, but it is difficult to get away from the point that in some of her novels and tales Miss McCarthy casts *too* cold an eye. One welcomes the feeling in *The Stones of Florence* for the Florentines themselves. The Venetians may have allowed their city to become a fairy tale, but the Florentines care for much more than their monuments, and Miss McCarthy has a fine scorn for the foreign residents in the past and present who have not been able to see this. And in *Memories of a Catholic Girlhood* she rises to a pitch of something like passion that makes it the noblest utterance that she has yet produced. One hopes for more in the future from the clear and eloquent voice that refused to make Pascal's wager in these biting terms: "Hence, as a lapsed Catholic, I do not trouble myself about the possibility that God may exist after all. If He exists (which seems to me more than doubtful), I am in for a bad time in the next world, but I am not going to bargain to believe in God in order to save my soul. Pascal's wager — the bet he took with himself that God existed, even though this could not be proved by reasoning — strikes me as too prudential. What had Pascal to lose by behaving as if God existed? Absolutely nothing, for there was no counter-Principle to damn him in case God didn't. For myself, I prefer not to play it so safe, and I shall never send for a priest or recite an Act of Contrition in my last moments. I do not mind if I lose my soul for all eternity. If the kind of God exists Who would damn me for not working out a deal with Him, then that is unfortunate. I should not care to spend eternity in the company of such a person."

INDEX

INDEX

For references within entries to each of the major novelists discussed in this volume initials only have been used, as for example SOJ for Sarah Orne Jewett

Adam Bede, 9, 69

Adams, Henry, 119

Addams, Frankie (fictional character), 165–66

African Genesis, 137

"After Holbein," 50

Age of Innocence, The, 5, 42–44, 45, 53, 114, 182

Alexander, Bartley (fictional character), 97–98

Alexander's Bridge, 97–98, 99, 102, 104

"All Souls," 34

Ambassadors, The, 44, 119, 164, 166

American Revolution, 17

Americans and American society, attitudes toward: of SOJ, 18; of EW, 25–26, 32, 38, 40, 47, 48–49, 53–54, 78, 83, 109, 130, 175; of EG, 73, 78, 79, 81, 82, 83, 109, 175; of WC, 109, 110, 111, 118; of EMR, 130, 175; of JS, 159; of MM, 174, 175, 178, 182, 184. *See also* Society and social classes

Americans in Europe, literary theme, use of: by EW, 32, 37, 38, 40–41, 44, 45–46, 48, 50, 52–53; by WC,

107–8, 118; by KAP, 143–45; by JS, 160

Ancient Law, The, 67, 87

Andrews, Wayne, 23

Andromaque, 167

"Angel at the Grave, The," 24

Anna Karenina, 7

April Twilights, 94

Archbald, Jenny Blair (fictional character), 80–81

Archer Newland (fictional character), 42–44

Ardrey, Robert, 137

Aristophanes, 180

Aristotle, 177

Arizona, 96, 101

Arnold, Matthew, 10

Aspern Papers, The, 13

Atlantic, 7, 10

Auden, W. H., 163

Auschwitz, 184

Austen, Jane, 7, 13, 18

"Autre Temps," 41

B——, Gerald, 57, 65, 75

Babbitt, George F. (fictional character), 4, 175, 178

189